Zoho CRM Essentials:

Mastering Zoho CRM
By Karen S. Fredricks

Technical Editor: Michelle Scott

Copy Editor: Gary Kahn

Other Works by Karen S Fredricks

- Act! 6 for Dummies
- Act! 2005 for Dummies
- Act! 2006 for Dummies
- Act! 2007 for Dummies
- Act! by Sage for Dummies
- SugarCRM for Dummies
- Microsoft Office Live for Dummies
- Microsoft Office Small Business Marketing Tips for Dummies
- Outlook 2007 Business Contact Manager for Dummies
- Outlook 2007 All in One for Dummies
- Outlook 2010 All in One for Dummies
- Sage Act! 2011 Reports and Dashboards Cookbook
- Sage Act! 2012 Cookbook
- Act! 2010 LinkedIn Learning video course
- Outlook 2010 LinkedIn Learning video course
- Outlook 2010 Essentials LinkedIn Learning video course

Copyright © Karen S. Fredricks 2021. All rights reserved.

Without limiting the rights under copyright(s) reserved below, no part of this eBook or print publication may be reproduced, stored in or introduced into a retrieval system, or transmitted, in any form, or by any means (electronic, mechanical, photocopying, recording, or otherwise) without the prior permission of the publisher and the copyright owner.

The content of this book is provided "AS IS." The Publisher and the Author make no guarantees or warranties as to the accuracy, adequacy or completeness of or results to be obtained from using the content of this book, including any information that can be accessed through hyperlinks or otherwise, and expressly disclaim any warranty expressed or implied, including but not limited to implied warranties of merchantability or fitness for a particular purpose. This limitation of liability shall apply to any claim or cause whatsoever whether such claim or cause arises in contract, tort, or otherwise. In short, you, the reader, are responsible for your choices and the results they bring.

The scanning, uploading, and distributing of this book via the internet or via any other means without the permission of the publisher and copyright owner is illegal and punishable by law. Please purchase only authorized copies, and do not participate in or encourage piracy of copyrighted materials. Your support of the author's rights is appreciated.

ISBN: 978-1-64457-275-7 (eBook)
ISBN: 978-1-64457-276-4 (Paperback)

ePublishing Works!
644 Shrewsbury Commons Ave
Ste 249
Shrewsbury PA 17361
United States of America
www.epublishingworks.com
Phone: 866-846-5123

Contents

Other Works by Karen S Fredricks
Dedication

Chapter 1

What in the World is Zoho? 1

    A Note from Your Geeky Sponsor 1
    What is a CRM? 2
    Pick Your Zoho Flavor 3
    Zoho CRM Modules vs Zoho Apps 4
    The Typical Zoho CRM User 4
    Some Basic Zoho CRM Ground Rules 5
    Converting, or Moving, to Zoho CRM 6
    Do You Speak Zoho? 7
    There's No Place Like Home 7

Chapter 2

Working with Contact Records 9

    Adding Records to Your Database 10
    Entering a New Record 11
    Leads Lead into Bigger Things 12
    Cloning a Contact 14
    The Contacts, They Are Changing 14
    Editing a Record 15
    Taking Account of Your Accounts 16

Seek and Ye Shall Find – And Change - Records 21

    Searching for That Special Someone 22

Filtering Records 23
　　A Room with a View 25
　　The Tabular View 25
　　Create a Canvas View 27
　　Kan You do the Kanban? 29
　　Create a Custom View 31
　　Doing the Global Find and Replace 33
　　Deduping Your Duplicates 36

Chapter 4

Please Stay in Touch 41
　　Zoho CRM is Up to the Task 42
　　Using the Zoho CRM Calendar for Scheduling a Meeting or
　　Time Sensitive Calls 45
　　Emailing Your Contacts 51
　　Pick Up the Phone and Dial 53

Chapter 5

You Can Have It Your Way 57
　　Setting up the System 57
　　Before You Start Modifying Your Database 58
　　Changing the Existing Database Fields 63
　　Adding a New Field 64
　　Manufacturing Custom Modules 70
　　Working with Subforms 73
　　Working with Layouts 75
　　Mapping Lead Fields for Conversion 80

Chapter 6

Batten Down the Hatches 81
　　Managing Database Users 81
　　Adding a New User to the Mix 88

Singing the Blueprint Blues 93
Data Administration for the Database Administrator 95

Chapter 7

Sending Email Blasts 101
Creating CRM Email Templates 102
Sending Templated Email 107
Campaigning Doesn't Just Occur in an Election Year 113

Chapter 8

Let's Make a Deal 115
Creating Multiple Pipelines 116
Customizing the Deal Stages 117
Modifying the Deal 120
Set up Big Deal Alert 121

Chapter 9

Show Me the Money 123
Adding Products Will Make You More Productive 124
You Can Quote Me on That 127

Chapter 10

I'm Between Projects Right Now 131
Creating a Project Is a Major Project 132
That Was Fun — Let's Do It Again! 139
Managing Your Projects 143

Chapter 11

Being Part of a Major Case Squad 147
State Your Case 148
Moving Up to Zoho Desk 149

Chapter 12

Viewing the Fruits of Your Labors 161
    I Need a New Home Page 161
    Tabbing Through Your Tabs 164
    Working with Reports 165
    Dashing Through the Dashboards 172

Chapter 13

ZohoPaloozza: Hacks & Shortcuts 177
    Add an Attachment to a Record 177
    Exporting Records 179
    Analyzing Things with Zoho Analytics 180
    We're Off to See the Wizard 180
    Creating a Webform 182
    Send a Survey 184
    Route it with RouteIQ 186
    Sometimes You Just Cliq with Someone 187

Chapter 14

I'd Like to Start with an App 191
    Zoho One 191
    You Can Take It with You 193
    Zoho Expense 194
    Begin with Bigin 194
    Adding Your Contacts to Your Mobile Device 195

Chapter 15

Help, Please 197
    Start by Taking a Good Look at Yourself 197
    Join a Local Zoho Users Group (ZUG) 200

Become an Official Zoholic 200
Hire a Zoho Consultant 201
Develop a Sense of Community 201
Appendix
    Index.. 202
    About Karen Fredricks 205

Dedication

This book is dedicated to all of my clients who have worked with me over the years to make their businesses more profitable and efficient through the use of CRM software. I am especially thankful for those clients who took a chance and moved to Zoho; it helped me to see Zoho through the eyes of a seasoned user.

A special shout out goes to Geoff Boulden who has devoted hours of his time and been so generous in helping others. I know Charlie Watts is looking down at you with a big smile!

Thank you, Michelle Scott, for your great ideas and grammar skills!

To my daughters, Andi and Alyssa. I love you to the moon and back!

And finally, to Gary Kahn, my partner in any and all things. You rock and you are my rock!

What in the World is Zoho?

The easiest part of starting a new product is, well, starting. By buying this book you've made a great start. If you're brand new to CRM, I suggest reading this book from beginning to end. If you've been using another CRM product, or have used Zoho, this book will serve as a reference guide that can be used on an as-needed basis. Zoho CRM is a fairly easy product to master, but this book allows you to jump in and avoid some of the "gotchas" that might impede the process.

A Note from Your Geeky Sponsor

Nobody likes technical jargon, but in the course of showing you how to use Zoho CRM, I might end up lapsing into Geek Speak. I may use a handful of somewhat technical terms. I just can't avoid it. Becoming familiar with those terms now is less painful in the long run.

First things first. Zoho CRM is a **database** application. A database is a collection of information organized in such a way that the user of the database can quickly find desired pieces of information. Think of a database as an electronic filing system. Although most Zoho CRM users create a database of Contacts, some users develop Zoho CRM databases to collect information about things other than Contacts. For example, you might create a Zoho CRM database to catalog all the wine in your wine cellar.

Traditional databases are organized by *fields, records,* and *modules:*

Field: A *field* is a single piece of information. In databases, fields are the smallest units of information. A tax form, for example, contains a number of fields: One for your name, one for your Social Security number, one for your income, and so on. In Zoho CRM, you start with 50 separate fields for each individual contact.

Record: A *record* is one complete set of fields. In Zoho CRM, all the information that you collect that pertains to one individual contact is a *contact record*.

Module: A *module* is a collection of similar records. For example, the *Contacts module* contains all the records of the people who have spent money – or soon hope to spend money – with your company. The *Tasks module* is a collection of all your past, present and future activities.

What is a CRM?

Before we starting working with Zoho CRM, it's important to understand what we mean by "**CRM**." CRM stands for customer relationship management, and typically refers to any software that helps you to manage your customer relationships. From a sales perspective, it can mean things like inputting and tracking leads, then checking up on those leads, converting them to contacts, and ultimately to deals. From a management perspective, you can track the progress of your sales team, create and run reports, and gather insights for your sale cycles and forecasts. Simply stated, the goal of any CRM product is to run your business efficiently, effectively, and to increase profitability.

Businesses without a good CRM tool are usually bogged down with complicated, messy, and time-consuming spreadsheets. Interoffice communication consists of sending email, picking up the phone or yelling across the room. Reminders consist of scribbled notes on a legal pad and dozens of sticky notes. Zoho CRM consolidates all of those processes. And because Zoho CRM is cloud based, your information always at your fingertips, from any web connected device. Another bonus of cloud based: it's always up-to-date.

CRM Software provides tools to manage business relationships by providing the ability to:

- ➢ Store complete contact information, including name, company, phone numbers, mailing addresses, and e-mail addresses.
- ➢ Record dated notes for each of your contacts so that you

can easily keep track of important conversations and activities. This feature is particularly useful for those of us who forget things on occasion.
- ➢ Keep a calendar that is cross-referenced with the appropriate contact so that you have a full record of all interactions that you've had - or will have - with a contact.
- ➢ Access reports and dashboards so that you can glean insight into your business based on the information in your database.
- ➢ Merge your contact information into templates that you create for marketing campaigns and other purposes. You can send those merged documents via snail mail, fax, or e-mail.
- ➢ Manage your sales pipeline with built-in forecasting tools.

Great CRM Software like Zoho CRM takes the concept of CRM a few steps farther by allowing for customization of every inch of the software and the ability to offer integration with virtually every aspect of your business.

Pick Your Zoho Flavor

Zoho CRM comes in four separate editions. Just about every feature found in the Enterprise version is also found in the Standard and Professional versions. The main difference is database size limits, the number of mass mails you can send per day, and the price. Let's take a look:

Free Edition – As the name implies, this version won't cost you a red cent. However, the database cannot be customized and does not allow for mass email.

Standard Edition – This version is $18/user/month ($12 if you pay annually) and lets you add up to 10 custom fields. With a Standard account you can send 250 mass emails/day.

Professional Edition - This model is $30/user/month ($20 if paid annually) and allows you to add up to 155 custom fields. With a Standard account you can send 500 mass emails/day.

Enterprise Edition - This edition is $45/user/month ($35 if paid annually) and you can add over 300 custom fields per module. With an Enterprise account you can send 1000 mass emails/day.

You can sign up for a trial of CRM here: ***TechBenders.com/ZohoCrm.***

If your budget is small, you can start with the Free, or Standard CRM, version and upgrade as your business, and wallet, grow

I am a big Zoholic so I highly recommend trying a Zoho One trial. The Zoho One platform can run most, if not all, of your business. Zoho One includes the Enterprise editions of all the applications. If you opt for Zoho One, you receive all the functionality of Zoho CRM Enterprise Edition.

In addition to Zoho CRM, you'll be able to investigate a variety of other business applications that are included with Zoho One including:

- Zoho Books: accounting app similar to QuickBooks
- Zoho Cliq: Zoho's app for instant messaging
- Zoho Meetings: conduct "Zoom" like meetings
- Zoho Sign: collect electronic signatures

At the end of the trial, you can either continue with Zoho One or opt just to continue with CRM. If you want to try all of the Zoho apps, sign up for a trial of Zoho One at **TechBenders.com/One.**

Once you sign up for your Zoho account you'll access the CRM portion by going to ***CRM.Zoho.com***.

Zoho CRM Modules vs Zoho Apps

This book focuses on the Zoho Modules (collections of similar records) within Zoho CRM. However, from time to time I illustrate the Zoho Apps that include additional functionality and require either additional costs, or a Zoho One subscription. Those Apps include:

Zoho Desk: The big brother application that corresponds to Zoho CRM's Case module.

Zoho Campaigns: The big brother application that corresponds to Zoho CRM's email functionality.

Zoho Projects: The big brother application that takes basic activities to a whole new level..

The Typical Zoho CRM User

So, who is the typical Zoho CRM user? Well, with more than 50 million registered Zoho users, you're safe to assume that nearly every industry is represented among its user base. Although Zoho started primarily as a tool for salespeople wanting to follow up on their prospects and customers, Zoho has evolved into a tool used by any individual or business trying to organize the chaos of daily business life.

- A CEO uses Zoho CRM because he wants to know what decisions to make by analyzing the data, how successful his his salespeople are doing, and how his customers are being treated.
- An administrative assistant uses Zoho CRM to automate routine tasks and to keep a schedule of various tasks and activities.
- A salesperson uses Zoho CRM to make sure that she's following up on all her prospects.
- A disorganized person uses Zoho CRM to help him become more organized.
- A smart person uses Zoho CRM because she knows that she'll have more time to play, by working more efficiently.
- A lazy person uses Zoho CRM because he knows it's more fun to play than to work.

Not to be a name dropper, but, Zoho CRM users include customers such as Amazon, Netflix and Facebook. They include business owners who run a solo company, Fortune 100 companies, and anyone in between.

- Large businesses that want to improve communication among employees.
- Small businesses that have to rely on a small staff to complete a multitude of tasks.
- Businesses of all sizes looking for software that can automate their business, and make them more productive in less time.
- Businesses looking to grow by marketing to their prospects.
- Businesses looking to retain their current customers, by providing an excellent level of customer service, and developing lasting relationships.

Some Basic Zoho CRM Ground Rules

Sometimes you just need to figure out things the hard way. After all, experience is the best teacher. Luckily for you, I've compiled a list of rules based on a few mistakes that I see other Zoho CRM users commit. You're not going to find these rules written down anywhere else, and they might not even make a whole lot of sense to you at the moment. However, as you become more and more familiar with Zoho CRM, these rules will be obvious.

Karen's Four Rules of Always:

- Always log in to Zoho CRM as yourself.
- Always strive for standardization in your database by entering your data in a consistent manner.
- Always input as much information into your database as possible.
- When in doubt, leave a field blank.

Converting, or Moving, to Zoho CRM

When you decide that Zoho CRM (or one of the other Zoho versions) is right for you, or you've already decided, but not yet set up Zoho in your office, moving everything from your system to another, can be tricky. This involves transferring all of your existing data, mapping it to the new locations, possibly creating new custom fields, and other important details.

Here are a couple of horror scenarios which, on the consulting end, I have heard about too many times. I am detailing them so you will avoid these frustrating, costly, and time-consuming mistakes.

ABC Company is extremely successful. They are a large manufacturer and outgrew their existing CRM, so they hired me to help with their conversion. The CEO is understandably quite busy, so he assigned his Admin Assistant to lead the project. The assistant, although quite capable and eager to please, lacked many of the skills necessary to lead a project of this magnitude. She had no access to their existing inventory system and had no familiarity with its usage. Her knowledge of email clients was limited to clicking the Send button in Outlook. She had no understanding of how the sales department worked and more importantly of their CRM requirements. And, her technical skills were such that she had no idea of her own CRM credentials, including her password.

XYZ Company is equally successful. Joe Senior (referred to as Senior) built the company from scratch and was grooming Joe Junior (aka Junior). to take his place. Senior put Junior in charge of the CRM migration to their new CRM program, i.e., Zoho. Junior knew nothing about their existing CRM system, or about CRM systems in general. So Junior hired an outside IT company that knew nothing about the old system, the new system, or about Junior and Senior's Company for that matter. A month later Senior Joe, Sr. was upset to learn that the project had still not gotten off the ground.

I could easily share dozens of similar stories. The bottom line is that when you decide Zoho CRM, or any one of their modules is the right product for your company, I urge you to hire an experienced and great consultant to help you with your CRM move (in geek speek it's called migration), or, conversion to Zoho CRM. To help the consultant, choose a thorough employee, with a full understanding of your company. It's a partnership; without it, your CRM migration is doomed.

Do You Speak Zoho?

You're going to be covering a lot of territory throughout this book about CRM and Zoho One features. Whether you are reading this book from beginning to end, or jumping around as needed, there are both a Table of Contents and an Index.

For starters, familiarize yourself with a few key terms:

Modules Bar: The line of items that appears at the top of the screen and starts with the CRM logo.

Left Navigation Bar: The line of choices that runs down the left side of Zoho CRM.

Setup Gear: The monkey wrench that appears in the top right-hand corner.

Profile: This might take the shape of your picture or a blank silhouette. Either way, it will allow you to see your Zoho account number as well as your name, in case you forgot it.

There's No Place Like Home

The first thing you'll see when you open Zoho CRM is the Home page. The Home page is totally customizable; you can learn how to change it in Chapter 12.

The best way to really learn Zoho CRM is by exploring.

Once you search around to find a function a couple of times, it should it should be tattooed in your brain. To that end, be on the lookout for these two icons; they both lead you to more options about the particular area you are in. And no, you won't break anything by clicking on them!

Zoho CRM Essentials

> **Ellipsis Button** (three dots).
> *Drop down Arrow:*

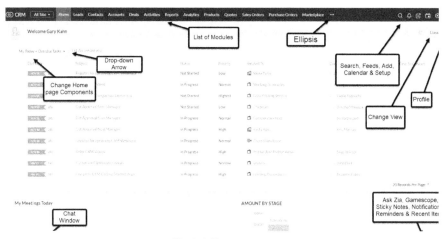

Fig 1-1 Home page

Working with Contact Records

In Zoho CRM, there are three basic types of contact records:

> **Leads** – a Lead is a person or organization with whom you are hoping to do business. As you build the relationship you can convert a lead to an Account, Contact or Deal.

> **Contacts** – a Contact is an individual person. They may be someone that has either purchased something in the past or shows interest in doing business with you now. They may be a vendor or contractor. The key is, Contacts are people in your database.

> **Accounts** – an Account is basically a company or organization record. In general, your business does business with other businesses - unless of course you mind your business and don't do business with anyone else! Several **Contact records** may be associated with one **Account Record.**

Zoho CRM makes a distinction between a **Lead** and a **Contact** record. In Zoho CRM-speak, a *Lead* is someone that has icicles hanging from his forehead - or at least hasn't started speaking with you in a warm and fuzzy manner about purchasing your products or services. A **Contact,** on the other hand, is someone you feel you have a great shot at closing or maybe they're someone you've already had some dealings with. In any case, you can always promote a **Lead** into a **Contact** as the snow starts to melt from his checkbook.

Zoho CRM Essentials

A database is only as good as the data it contains. In Zoho CRM, adding, deleting, and editing the records in your database is easy. In this chapter, you'll learn how to do all three of these tasks in order to maintain an organized, working database. Fortunately for you, the same processes apply to Leads, Contacts, and Accounts.

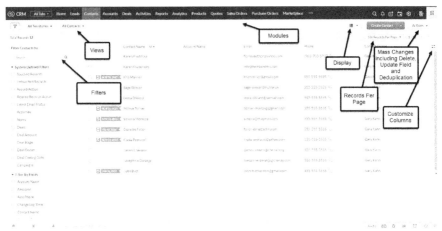

Fig 2 -1 The List View

Adding Records to Your Database

There's more than one road that leads to Rome, and more than one way to get records into Zoho CRM. The quickest way to add records is by following one of these methods:

➢ Import leads from a spreadsheet in CSV or XLSX format

➢ Capture leads from your website with a Zoho CRM Webform

However, Rome wasn't built in a day and neither is your Zoho CRM database. Some of you will have to do it the hard way: by manually entering your lead data. This may help incentivize you to create a few Lead forms, or to search your hard drive for missing spreadsheets!

Working with Contact Records

Fig 2-2 Contact Detail View

Entering a New Record

1. Click the appropriate **module** in Zoho CRM's top **Navigation bar**.

2. Click the **Plus** icon to the left of the Import icon on the far-right side of your screen.

3. In the **Create (module)** page, enter the details.

    You'll want to fill in as many of the juicy details as possible. If you are missing information for a field, it's better to leave it blank than to fill it with unnecessary garbage.

4. Click **Save**. If your Zoho CRM Administrator decided to get fancy, you might be nagged to fill in missing, required information. Those required fields are highlighted in red. Go ahead, fill in that information and make your Administrator happy!

Fig 2-3 Entering a New Rcord

Leads Lead into Bigger Things

Zoho CRM has a fairly systematic way of looking at your -day-to-day business. The theory is that Zoho CRM does everything in its power to help you collect Leads. Then, once the magic begins and you start to gauge some level of interest, Zoho CRM provides you with a very easy way to convert those Leads to Contacts, Accounts, and/or Deal records. This magic happens with a simple click of the Convert button.

Once you've mastered the Leads module, you are ready to branch out to the Contacts, Accounts, and Deals modules. Lucky for you, all the same rules apply. You can add and edit records to any of these modules using the same methodology you used to add and edit Leads. But, because the Contacts, Accounts, and Deals are a little more important – or at least represent a few more bucks in your pockets – you might find yourself requiring a few more bells and whistles. No problem, Zoho CRM is more than up to the challenge.

You start with an icy cold Lead, call them a few times and then miracle of miracles: they are ready to do business! Zoho CRM lets you convert a Lead into an Account, Contact, and/or a Deal. You can even map the Lead fields to those of the Account, Contact, and Deals. Those mapped fields are transferred to the new records, saving you the time of reentering data.

To convert a Lead:

1. **Search** for the Lead record.

2. Click **Convert** in the **Lead Details** page.

   Zoho CRM will make suggestions for the new Contact and Account name, or suggest already existing ones if it finds a match.

3. (Optional) Select the **Create a new Deal for this Account** checkbox if you also want to create a new Deal record based on this lead. If you choose this option, all the mandatory fields for the Deals module will be listed:

   - ✓ **Amount**
   - ✓ **Deal Name:** By default, the *Account Name* will be populated as the deal name. Best practice is to add a bit more detail as a reminder of what the Deal is. For instance, *ABC Company – Zoho CRM Project*.
   - ✓ **Closing Date:** This is just a guesstimate, but helps you prioritize the Deal.
   - ✓ **Stage:** You'll notice that your company's stages appear in the drop-down list.
   - ✓ **Contact Role:** Sometimes the person you have been dealing with is NOT the actual decision maker and you might want to make note of that factoid.
   - ✓ **Campaign Source:** You'll notice that you can tie a deal directly to a previous campaign effort. This data isn't required, but is helpful in tracking sales ROI or the effectiveness of specific sales and marketing efforts. So if you know where it came from, enter it!
   - ✓ **Owner of the record:** You only need to change this if someone other than YOU is in charge of the Deal.

4. Click **Convert.** Zoho CRM immediately presents you with the hyperlinks to the new Account and Contact records. Oh, and by the way, the original Lead record is gone, but not forgotten.

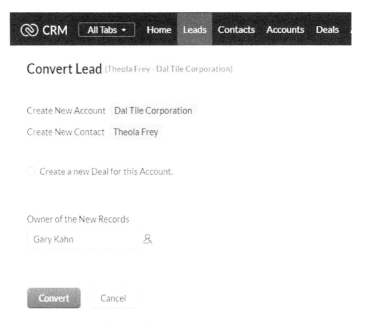

Fig 2-4 Converting a Lead

Cloning a Contact

From time to time you may feel the urge to duplicate a contact. For example, you might have a new contact at an existing company and the two contacts will be identical, except for some very minor changes. Adding another contact to an existing account is always a good option, but all of the account fields might not be mapped to the Contact fields. Or maybe you just want to create the new Contact while you are viewing an existing contact, rather than having to access the account record.

Here's all you need to do to clone a Contact:

1. Access the **Contact record** you wish to clone.
2. Click the **Ellipsis** Button on the **Contact Details** page and select **Clone**.
3. Modify any details in the **Clone Contact** page.
4. Click **Save**.

The Contacts, They Are Changing

Companies relocate and change their names, people move, and your fingers sometimes slip on the keyboard. People change e-mail addresses. All these predicaments require the editing of records. Don't worry; changing the information in Zoho CRM is as easy as entering it. And, you can make changes in a variety of ways. For now, we are sticking to making changes one Contact at a time. In the next chapter you'll learn how to make global changes.

Editing a Record

Once you have created a record, you can sit back and admire your handiwork – at least until you realize that something needs to be changed. Maybe you noticed an input error, or maybe you just need to add a few more pearls of wisdom.

You can **edit** contacts in **Zoho CRM** in a number of ways, depending on where you are in Zoho CRM and how much information you want to change.

Tweaking Single Fields

There are times you spot a field or two that need changing as you're perusing a record. This can be easily done.

1. **Click** on the record you wish to change from the appropriate **module**.
2. Hover the cursor over the field you wish to change; you'll see a **pencil icon** magically appear.
3. **Click** the **Pencil** icon and make your change.
4. **Click** the **Checkmark** to save your change.

Changing the Entire Record

Although clicking in and changing a field or two is handy, making major changes can be a bit daunting – especially if you forget to keep checking that little blue checkbox to save each change. If you need to make multiple changes, you might find it easier to do so from the ***Edit record mode.***

Like a lot of other functions in Zoho CRM, there are a few ways to get to the **Edit record** page:

- ➢ Search for and select the record for editing
- ➢ In the list or Tabular View, hover over the record and click the **Pencil** icon to the left of the record.
- ➢ Click on the record name in the Tabular View.

Once on the record, edit it by:

1. Click the **Edit** button. The record opens in full **Edit mode**. You are now free to change any and all fields, depending on your permissions.

2. Click **Save** to save your changes.

Deleting a Single Record

What if you simply need to delete a record? Maybe you are no longer do business with one of your contacts or they've gone out of business. For whatever reason you decide that a record no longer needs to be a part of your database, you can just delete it.

The good news is that it's easy to delete a record. The bad news is that it is ridiculously easy to delete a record. Not to worry. If you mistakenly delete a record, Zoho CRM stores that record in the Recycle Bin for 60 days. Just as easily as the record was accidentally deleted, it can be restored.

Like editing the record, there is more than one way to delete a record.

1. From the Global Search option, find the desired record.
2. Click on the record to Open it.
3. Click the **Ellipsis** button in the right side of the **Record** page
4. Click **Delete**.
5. Click the big red **Delete** button on the popup message.
6. Bid adieu to the deleted record.

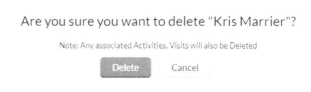

Fig 2-5 Deleting a Record

Taking Account of Your Accounts

Your database might contain the names of the head guy (also

known as The Decision Maker), your main point of contact (the guy who signs the checks) and the person who does all the work (the Administrative Assistant). Seems easy at first, until the head guy gets fired, the check-signer takes off for Brazil, and new people replace them both.

Accounts are collections of your Contact records, usually within one company. An Account may be a company or an organization. A Contact can belong to only one Account. Accounts allow you to track of all the activity associated with the Contacts within those Accounts. This helps to eliminate "who said what to whom," as all interactions can be easily viewed from one centralized Account record.

Account or the Contact? You might wonder which type of records you should add to your database first. You might want to start by adding your Accounts; you'll be able to associate any new Contact records to them as you enter them. Or, you might think it makes more sense to add a Contact and create the Account from there.

There are a lot of similarities between the Contact and Account portions of Zoho CRM. You can apply most of the concepts that you know about Contacts to Accounts.

For example:

- ✓ You can customize your Account module fields and associated drop-down lists.
- ✓ You can add Account-specific Notes, Attachments, Activities, and Deals.

Associating an Existing Contact with an Existing Account

From time to time, you might find that a contact is not associated with an existing Account. Or perhaps the Contact was associated with an *incorrect* Account. Either way, this is simple to correct.

To associate a Contact to a different Account:

1. Use the **Global Search** option to find and select the Contact.
2. Click the **Pencil** icon in the **Account Name** field.
3. Enter the Account Name. If the Account exists, the name auto-populates. Click it to associate the **Contact** to the **Account**.
4. If the Account does not exist, click the **New Account** button

and fill in the **Quick Create** view. Remember to fill in the rest of the details later.

5. Click the **Blue checkmark** to save.

Fig 2-6 Associating a Contact to an Account

Some Companies Need a Parent

In a typical business scenario, an **Account** represents a Company with which your organization does business, or is planning to do business with in the future. An Account stores the company address, number of employees, annual revenue, and other pertinent details.

In really large companies (generally those that have their own cafeteria and a lot of cubicles), various **divisions** or locations can result in a complex hierarchy. For example, you might work with a company that has many stores or branches. You may need to need handle each one individually. Fortunately, Zoho CRM can accommodate your need to track contacts, companies, and even divisions.

In Zoho CRM, you can create a "parent-child" relationship between a company and its various divisions. The "main" company record is considered the **Parent Account**; the divisions are **Member Accounts.** You can create a Member Account directly from the Parent Account and view the individual Member Accounts directly from the Parent Account.

You might wonder whether you should attach a Contact record to the Parent Account or the Member Account. A good rule of thumb is to attach the Contact record to the Account or division that you

Working with Contact Records

are actually working with. If you need to associate a Contact to multiple Accounts, you can do this by creating a multi-select lookup field.

There are two important rules to remember when associating a Member Account to a Parent Account:

> ➢ The **Member Accounts Related List** only allows you to add **new** subdivisions. You cannot associate an existing Account record to the Parent Account from the Parent Account.

> ➢ If you want to associate an existing Account to a Parent Company, you do so from the Member Account record.

Adding a Member Account to an Existing Account Record

When you start building an Account hierarchy, the best practice is to create the Parent Account first, and then add the divisions or Member Accounts second.

Here's an easy way to create an Account hierarchy:

1. Search for and select the **Account record.**

2. Click **Member Accounts** in the **Related List** area. You will be transported to the Member Accounts area. If any exist, you'll see them listed here.

3. Click the **New** icon. The **Create Account** page will open.

4. Fill in the pertinent details about the Member Company. You'll notice that the Parent Account field is already populated with the name of the existing account.

5. Click **Save**. The new division is now listed in the **Member Accounts** list of the Parent Account.

6. You can also hover over the **Member Company Related List** and click the **Plus** icon.

Fig 2-7 Creating an Account Hierarch

Associating Existing Accounts to the Parent Account

It's not unusual to find that a company you are working with is actually a sub-division or subsidiary of an existing Account. As stated earlier, you can't associate an existing Account to a Parent Account from the Parent Account record itself, but you can easily convert an existing Account to a Member Account.

Here's all you need to do:

1. Search for and select the **Account Record** that you would like to morph into a Member Account.
2. Click in the **Parent Account** field.
3. Type in and select the **Parent Account** from the picklist.
4. Click the **Checkmark** button to save.

Your Account is now associated as a Member Account to the Parent Account. As a bonus you can click the Parent Account hyper-link to navigate the hierarchy and get to the Parent Account.

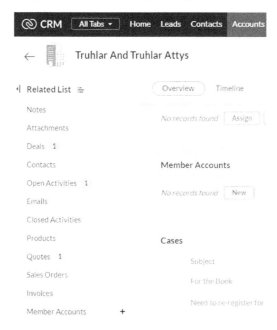

Fig 2-8 Member Accounts Related List

Seek and Ye Shall Find – And Change - Records

If all roads lead to Rome, surely all processes in Zoho CRM lead to the *Search page*. A *search* is a way to focus on a specific a portion of your database, depending on your specifications. A good practice in Zoho CRM is to perform a search first and then perform an action second. For example, you might perform a search and then follow up on your key opportunities. Or you might do a search and then perform a mail merge.

The theory behind the search is that you don't always need to work with all your contacts at one time. Not only is working with only a portion of your database easier, at times, doing so is absolutely necessary. If you're changing your mailing address, you probably want to send a notification to everyone in your database. However, if you're running a special sales promotion, you might want to target specific Leads and/or Contacts. If you're sending holiday gift baskets, you probably want the names of only your very best customers.

In Zoho CRM you can *search* for information across all modules or *filter* records in a specific module by a single field, or by several fields. You can create and save your filters if you find you are consistently looking at the same subset of records. Or, if you find you need to look at specific fields with different records, you can create a *Custom View*, which filters and displays your records in a preset format.

Searching for That Special Someone

Global Search allows you to search all of your Zoho CRM database

to find just the item you're looking for. For instance, if you are looking for the details of a Contact named Bob, but can't remember his last name, you could search for "Bob". When searching for an Account, type.

Type part of the Account name in the Global Search and Zoho CRM finds you a match. Let's say you can't remember either the person or company name, but you remember that some of a conversation was about soccer. If you put soccer into a Note, searching for "soccer" would lead you back to the right person.

Here's all you need to do to perform a search:

1. Click the **Search** icon in the far-right side of the **Horizontal Navigation Bar.**

2. **Enter** your search criterion.

3. (Optional) If you see the item you are looking, **click** it. As you type, you'll notice that items begin to appear in the search area, separated by module.

4. Hit the **Enter** key to open the **Search page**. The Search page displays a list of all matching records, segmented by module.

5. (Optional) Click the small arrow near the **Search** icon and select specific modules to filter the search results based on modules.

6. (Optional) Check the **Show only my records** checkbox to show only those records for which you are listed as the record owner.

7. Click on the desired record or click the **X** in the top-right corner to close the **Search** page.

Seek and Ye Shall Find – And Change - Records

Fig 3-1 The Search Page

Filtering Records

In the previous section you learned how to search for a single record. More often than not though, you do not want to view all of your data at the same time. For example, you may be interested in only viewing the Leads created during the last week, or you may want to only view the Deals in a specific stage. The best way to handle these scenarios is to filter your records.

Zoho CRM allows you to filter your records based on any of the fields for that record type, or based on the Activities associated to the records, including email status, Activities and Deals. Your filter can be based on a single field value. For example, you could filter for all Leads whose state is "California". You can also create more sophisticated queries such as Leads "that have no open Activities," or "Deals without any Notes for the last 6 months".

Here's all you need to know to create a filter:

1. **Click** on the desired module.
2. Type the name of a field in the **Filter Contacts By** Search box.
3. Select as many fields as you like. You can scroll down the list of options in the **Vertical Navigation Bar.** or type the name of a field in the magnifying-glass area.
4. Add the criteria for each field you select.

Zoho CRM Essentials

Your search parameters depend on the field(s) you select. For example, if you select Notes, you can choose whether to search for records with or without notes, and even a specific time range. If you select a field that is associated with a picklist, you are presented with only those options.

5. Click **Apply Filter**. The records that meet your criteria are displayed.

6. Click **Save Filter** if you would like to use the filter again in the future. The **Save Filter** popup window opens.

7. Name the Filter and click Save.

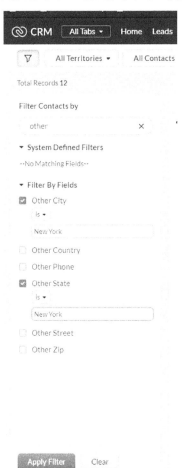

Fig 3-2 Filtering Records

Once saved, the filter is listed among your other saved filters. The number of records in the filter appears to the right of the Filter's name;

the count is updated in real-time. Saved filters are specific to each user, and each user can only save a maximum of 5 filters.

A Room with a View

Viewing your records is very easy. Just click the desired module on Zoho CRM's **Horizontal Navigation Bar**. Zoho CRM has three basic views for your viewing pleasure.

> ➢ *Tabular View:* The Tabular View displays the records in a table format. Each record is represented by a line in the table, while the columns represent specific fields in the module. Click on a hyperlink to drill down to the detail view. Generally, the Tabular View should be limited to nine fields or less, to avoid horizontal scrolling.

> ➢ *Kanban View:* "Kanban" is Japanese for "card that you can see." You might not think the Kanban makes much sense for basic records. However, it is also a great view to use when working with Deals as you can "drag and drop" the Kanban "tiles" from one category to the next.

> ➢ *Canvas View*: Your name might not be Picasso, but that doesn't mean that you aren't creative. The Canvas View allows you to design your very own way of looking at your records.

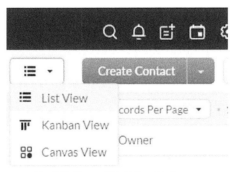

Fig 3-3 Record List View Options

The Tabular View

The *Tabular View* is simply a list of records arranged by Columns and Rows similar to what you would see in a spreadsheet. By default, the Tabular View provides you with eight columns. As a bonus, you see the total count of all your records on the bottom left corner of the Tabular View page. You can get to the Tabular View by clicking the Tabular View icon on the right-side of the Navigation Bar of any module.

Getting to the Tabular View is only half the fun. The other half comes from seeing some of the cool things that you can accomplish by using the Tabular View.

Zoho CRM provides a set of ***Standard list views*** that are ready to be used by all the users in your organization. You can modify the Standard Views and sort the order of the columns in the list. However, you cannot delete these list views.

You can choose one of the Standard list views by selecting one of the views from the View drop-down list located at the far-left side of the module's Navigation Bar.

Changing the Columns in the Tabular View

These eight columns may be all you need to scroll through your contacts. However, there may be times when you want to see additional information. For example, let's say you sell service plans and want to see the expiration dates. It's easy to change columns as well as reorder of the columns by following these steps:

1. Click the **Manage Column** button in the upper left-hand corner of the **List View**. The **Manage Columns** popup opens.

2. Type the **name** of the desired field(s) in the Search box or **scroll** through the list of fields.

   Click in the **Checkbox** next to the field name(s) to choose the columns you'd like to appear in the **Tabular View**.

   You might want to limit yourself to nine columns when deciding which fields you want to view in the Tabular View; if you select too many fields, you'll have to do some horizontal scrolling to see all of your fields.

3. (Optional) In the **Column selector** window, hover your mouse over any field and drag the field to a new location to change the order of the columns.

4. Click Save to save your changes.

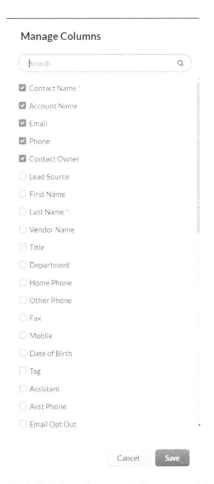

Fig 3-4 Selecting Columns for the Tabular View

Sorting Records in Tabular View

Records in the Tabular View can be sorted in ascending or descending order with literally a click of a button. Click any column heading and select the **Ascending** or **Descending** option and voila. With the ascending option, any have blank records appear at the top of the list. If you choose the Ascending option.

Create a Canvas View

Arranging fields the way you want them to appear might sound like a no-brainer, but it's easy to forget the importance of strategically changing the field locations in a View. For example, you might choose a layout that has the main business phone number on the top portion of your layout, the home phone number on a different tab along the bottom, and the mobile phone number in a third location. If you're constantly flipping around records to find key pieces of information, you can move them together into one strategic place. The point is that you can design a Canvas View in such a way that makes it easy to view your data.

With Canvas View you can create a view that is truly unique to the way you work. For example, you might want to scroll through your contacts and see specific key pieces of information. The Tabular View only lets you see eight fields at a time horizontally. Canvas View lets you design the way you want your records to be displayed, and there are no restrictions on how you want to display this data. You can add pictures, use custom buttons, and choose different font colors, font sizes, and alignments. You can also group fields and display them in any order you like. Additionally, if your business is multi-faceted you can create more than one canvas.

You can create your own Canvas View from scratch, or choose one of the predefined templates which can be and customized as much as you like.

Here's how you can begin to create your first masterpiece:

1. Select the desired module.

2. Click the **Canvas View** icon. You are redirected to the **Canvas View** page.

3. Click **Create Your First Canvas View** to continue.

    You have two options here. **Blank Template** lets you build your own canvas view from scratch. Alternatively, you can scroll through samples which are categorized on the left-hand side of the screen. You might want to start with a pre-designed template. You can customize it, and it you be spared a lot of tedious setup work. If you decide to start from scratch skip to Step 5.

4. Select each field and choose the corresponding field from the drop-down list to map the fields in the **Canvas** to your actual Zoho CRM fields. Any fields that you do not map will not appear in the final Canvas.

5. Click **Next** to continue. The **Canvas List View Builder** page opens. You'll notice all your database fields listed along the left-hand side.

6. **Drag and drop** the desired fields onto the **Canvas View**.

Remember, you are creating a way to preview your records. Organize the fields in a way that makes sense to you; change fonts and add color, resize fields, line up fields. The sky is the limit.

7. Click the **Preview** button to view your efforts. The preview is a fairly accurate representation of the final Canvas.
8. Click **Save** if you are happy with your work of art.
9. Enter a **name** for the Canvas View created and indicate which users will be allowed to share it.
10. Click **Save** to save your changes.

Fig 3-5 Creating a Canvas View

Congratulations! You are now the proud owner of your very own, customized Canvas View. If you want, you can add additional Canvas Views for each module.

Kan You do the Kanban?

The Tabular View lists all records, one after the other. By contrast, the Kanban view is much more graphical. The Kanban View is a "card-based" view that divides your data into vertical categories. Each card represents a record in your database; instead of viewing your contacts line by-line, you can view them side by side. If you're a person who likes to view rather than to visualize, this view is for you!

The neat thing about the Kanban View is that you can easily rearrange your cards by dragging them to another vertical category. For example, you can categorize your Leads based on the status field or arrange your Deals based on their sales stage. If a record changes status, you can simply drag their card to a different column.

You can use one of the pre-designed Kanbans, or you can create one entirely from scratch:

1. Go to the **Module** (leads, contacts, accounts, etc.) for which you want to create a new Kanban View.

2. Click the **Kanban View** icon on the far-right side of the **Horizonal Navigation Bar**. The **Kanban View – Settings** popup window opens.

3. Fill in the following details in the **Kanban View Settings** popup window:

    ✓ **Kanban View Name:** You can create various Kanban views so give this one a good name.

    ✓ **Categorized By:** This is generally a picklist field. If you are creating a Kanban View for Deals you might base it on Sales Stage; if it's based on Leads you might choose the Lead Source field.

    ✓ (Optional) **Aggregate By:** Depending on the module you are asked for the aggregate field. This is generally a currency field and the Kanban View shows a total based on that field. Kanbans without the aggregate option simply gives a total for each column at the top of the Kanban.

    ✓ **Header Style:** Choose **Mono color** if you want the column headings to all be the same color, or **Random Colors** if you want each column to be a different color.

    ✓ **Select Fields:** Select the fields that you want to view within each record

4. Click **Save** to save your new Kanban View.

Fig 3-6 The Deal Kanban View

Create a Custom View

There is yet another trick up Zoho CRM's sleeve; you can save your filters and column preferences to one handy dandy Custom View.

As an example, let's say that you are tasked with two chores: one is to reach out to all of your customers with expiring service contracts or yearly software contracts, and the other is to stop by local prospects and pass out brochures. When dealing with the expiration dates, you need to access various Contact records and see their names, email addresses, various phone numbers, and their expiration dates. However, when dealing with the prospects you might prefer to see addresses and don't need to see expiration dates.

You can create, modify and delete Custom Views List Views. They are categorized by:

- **Favorites** - Views that you have marked as favorites are displayed.
- **Created by Me** - Custom views created by you (the user) are displayed.
- **Shared with Me** - Custom views explicitly shared with you by any user in your CRM account are displayed.
- **Public Views** - Views that are accessible to everyone in your CRM account are displayed.
- **Other Users' Views** - Custom views created by fellow users (usually co-employees) in your CRM account, which doesn't come under the above categories are displayed. **Only Administrators** can see the views created by other users.

Here's all you need to do to create a Custom View:

1. Click the **module tab** for which you would like to create a custom view.
2. Click the list view's drop-down in the top left side of the **Module's Homepage**.
3. Click the Create View link. The **New View** page opens.
4. Enter the **Custom View** name.
5. (Optional) **Click** the **Star** to mark the new view as a Favorite. This is helpful for Views you use often. Marking a

View as a Favorite floats it to the top of your View picklist.

6. Specify the search criteria to use to filter the records. You will now have a drop-down list with those time-saving parameters.

7. Select one of the operators in the operator field.

    This is how you will save yourself time and effort so make as many shortcuts as you can. Indicate whether you're looking for a specific word, a field that contains a part of a word, or even a range of figures or dates. You can search for fields that contain data, or for fields that are blank and don't contain any data.

8. (Optional) Click the **Plus** icon next to the first criterion to add another one.

9. (Optional) Click the **And** that is situated between each line of your criteria to clarify the relationship between each line of your criteria.

    When you build the query, you might want to make use of the And/Or column to help you group your criteria to indicate the relationship between each set of criteria. For example, if you are looking for record(s) that are located in California and Oregon you would use OR to indicate that a record needs to exist in only one of the states.

10. (Optional) Create a **Criteria Pattern**.

    Queries often make use of parentheses to group like items together. This is a particularly important step if your query contains both "and" and "or" criteria. You can add up to 25 criteria, so making sure they are properly grouped is imperative if you expect them to work.

11. **Select** the columns to be displayed in the module view.

    You can select a field from the **Available** list box by clicking the **Plus** icon to the right of the desired field. You can change the order of the items in the **Selected** list box by dragging a field to a new location, or remove an item by clicking the **Minus** icon to the right of an item.

12. Indicate whom, if anyone, to share this view in the **Share this with** section.

13. Click **Save**.

Seek and Ye Shall Find – And Change - Records

Fig 3-7 Creating a Custom View

Pat yourself on the back. Your several minutes of brilliance will be rewarded with a lifetime of saved time!

Doing the Global Find and Replace

Using picklists goes a long way to helping with data consistency, but you might notice large areas of data that need correcting. Or perhaps you need to make a personnel change and reassign a large group of records to a new employee. You can fix these records by correcting each field on an item-by-item basis, or you can query the records in question and change them all in one fell swoop. I know which option gets my vote!

I have two tidbits of advice for you before proceeding with either process. One is designed to save your time and the other is designed to save your butt.

➢ **Save Your Time:** Most of the time Zoho CRM is fairly intuitive. This is not one of those times. Let's say a filter for records in which the state field contains "fla" returns 2200 records. You can display 100 records per page. When you select the records, you can only select 100 at a time. Which means you will have to repeat the process 22 times. However, if you create a *Custom View*, you can magically select all 2200 records at one time.

➢ **Save Your Butt**: Unless you're planning on changing field data for *every* record, make sure you perform a *filter* prior to proceeding. These changes are irreversible! For example, say you notice 27 instances of *Fla* that you want to change to *FL*. If you fail to filter your records first, you'll end up changing the State field for *every* record in your current view to *FL*, rather than just for the original 27 that you intended to change. Unfortunately, unless you have a backup handy, you're stuck with the changes. These changes are irreversible.

Making Global Changes in the Tabular View

Once you've mastered the art of filtering your records, a whole new world of options opens up. And, they all start by selecting records which you can easily do by clicking the **Select** option which is to the left of the column headings.

➢ Set Reminder
➢ Mass Update
➢ Change Owner
➢ Add to Campaigns
➢ Update Response
➢ Print Mailing Labels
➢ Mail Merge
➢ Delete Contacts

As easy as these changes are to make there is one trick that makes this even easier. The **Select** button selects all of the displayed options, so if you are displaying 100 records per page you will be selecting 100 records. To select all records, click the **Select All records in this view** option.

Deleting Multiple Records Using the Tabular View

The only thing worse than making a mistake is making a whopper of a *mistake*. No problem Zoho; Zoho CRM can help clean up both your small and large messes. Here's how you can delete multiple records:

1. Create a Search for the records you want to delete. For example, if you realize after the fact that all the contacts you imported two months ago from the ABC Trade Show were entered incorrectly, then you would search for all records whose **Lead Source** is ABC Trade Show.

2. Click the **checkbox** displayed in the column header. If your contact view is set to display 100 records you will be selecting 100 records.

3. Click the **Ellipsis** button that appears and chose **Delete**.

4. Click the big red **Delete** button on the popup message.

Mass Update

Mass Update is designed to help you correct all of the information in a single field. For example, maybe some of your records have the city listed in all capitals, but others don't. Perhaps some records are listed in *Florida* whereas other contacts reside in *FL* or *Fla*. This lack of consistency makes it extremely difficult to query your database. Fortunately, it is extremely easy to fix.

1. Click the Module tab that you wish to correct and **filter** for the guilty records.

2. Click the **Select All** checkbox located at the top left corner of the **List View**.

3. Click the Ellipsis button and select **Mass Update**. The **Mass Update** popup window opens.

4. Select the field that you want to update from the **Select a field drop-down** and specify a value for the field. If you want to fix a bunch of errant states, select Mailing State from the drop-down and fill in FL as the value.

5. Click **Update**.

Fig 3-8 Mass Update a Field

Change Owner

Once you get the hang of filtering records, there are any number of changes that you can do globally. A common one is to change the ownership for various records. This scenario is common when one of your employees leaves your organization and is replaced by someone else. To mass change ownership:

1. Create a **filter** for the previous record owner.
2. Click the checkbox at the top of the view that **selects all records** in the list.
3. (Optional) **Click Select All in this view** to select more than a pageful of records.
4. Click the **Ellipsis** button and select **Change Owner**.
5. Select the name of the **new user**.
6. Click Change Owner.

You'll probably have to repeat this exercise for every module that the former employee touched (Deals, Leads, Activities, etc). Lucky for you, this can be done in a matter of minutes!

Deduping Your Duplicates

When you work with a significant amount of data, it gets quite challenging to keep your database free from duplicates. As the number of users in your database increases, and your processes become more sophisticated, so too does the likelihood of creating duplicates. For example, the same Lead may be created via import, via APIs, and through a rep that receives a new inquiry via phone. To help you manage a clean set of data, Zoho CRM offers both proactive and reactive solutions.

Remember: the best way to keep your dupes to a minimum is to not create them all. A quick search before creating a record can be a life saver. However, should you realize that a record exists multiple times in your database, you can easily merge them together.

By marking a certain field as a "unique field," you can stop the creation of a duplicate record. This is a proactive way to maintain a clean database. For example, if you have marked the phone number field as a unique field in the Leads module, Zoho CRM will alert you if you create a second lead with the same phone number as an existing lead.

Despite creating unique fields and double-checking data, if you still think there could be duplicate records in your CRM, you can use Zoho CRM's de-duplication tools to merge them.

Find and Merge Duplicates

One method of deduping involves working with a single set of duplicated records "on the fly." You can use this feature if you stumble upon a duplicate of a particular record. For example, you look up the name **Bob Anderson** and find that you have two or three of them lurking in your database.

Find and merge lets you merge duplicate records into a single record and delete the duplicates. The retained record is known as the **master record** and the deleted record as the **duplicate record**.

To merge a single set of duplicate records:

1. Open one of the records you suspect is duplicated.

   Click the **Ellipsis button** and choose **Find and Merge Duplicates**. The **Find and Merge Duplicate Contacts** page opens. The suggested matching criteria are displayed. In the **Search Criteria** section; any matching records appear in the appropriately titled **Matching Records** area at the bottom of the page.

2. (Optional) Remove any unwanted criteria by changing the operator to **None**; click **Search**.

3. In the **Matching Records** section, select at least two records to be merged and then click **Next**. You can merge a maximum of three records at a time. The **Deduplicate Contacts** page opens.

4. Select the record that you want to retain as the **Master Record**.

This part can look a bit scary at first. You need to decide which record to keep (Record 1) and which record receives the heave-ho (Record 2). You can change your preference by selecting the radio button at the top of each record.

5. Click the radio buttons near the corresponding fields for each record to determine which field values should be kept in case of a conflict. The final outcome appears in the Master Record column.

6. (Optional) Click **Select All** if you wish to merge all of the conflicting fields with the values from one specific record.

7. Click **Merge**. A very scary warning message appears, so look scared.

8. Click the **I understand Merge Now** button.

Fig 3-9 The Dedupe Screen

The duplicated record(s) are merged to the master record and permanently deleted; this process can't be reversed. Any attachments and activities from the deleted records are transferred to the new master record.

Auto Merging Duplicates

In the section above, you learned what to do if you come across a single set of duplicate records. However, finding that duplicate set of records might set your wheels turning. What if there were a way to search Zoho CRM for duplicate records based on unique fields such as a phone number or email address? Well, guess what my friend? There is a way.

The **Deduplication Contacts** feature runs a check on any module and *automatically* find and merge exact matches. And, in case of a conflict in field values, Zoho CRM prompts you to manually resolve the conflict.

Zoho CRM considers one record as a **master record** to run the duplicate check. This record is chosen based on the most recent activity. For example, if you have three records with the same email address, the record that has the most recent activity is automatically treated as the master record. The other two records are considered duplicate records, and be deleted. This occurs automatically and cannot be changed.

To merge duplicate records using the Deduplication tool:

1. Click the **Module** tab where you suspect there are duplicates lurking.

2. Click the **Ellipsis** button and select **Deduplicate Contacts**. The **Deduplicate Contacts** page opens. The de-duplication process can be initiated only by one user, per module, at a time.

3. Select the fields by which you would like to search for duplicate records. You can select up to three fields.

   Note that fields that you have marked as **unique fields** appear here. If you have not marked any unique fields, Zoho CRM displays a standard set of fields for the module. For example, you can select **Email** and Account Name if you want to find records that have both the same Account Name and the same company name. You can select a maximum of three fields at a time.

4. Click the **Find and Merge Duplicates** button. A popup window informing you of the basic ground rules appears.

5. Click **Yes, proceed** to continue.

   Hang tight. You are notified when the merge is finished. If the duplicates found by Zoho CRM are exact copies of each other, Zoho CRM automatically merges them and you are finished. However, if a conflict exists between the duplicates, you must resolve the conflict by manually merging the records.

6. (Optional) Resolve any conflicts by clicking one of the following options in the **Deduplicate Contacts** popup window.

- ✓ **Resolve Now** - When CRM opens a popup on the conflict, you can immediately resolve it by click **Resolve Now.** You can then select any of the records and merge them together following the same steps you used when merge single sets of duplicate contacts.

- ✓ **Do it later** - If you are busy with other activities, click **Resolve Later**. An email with the results of the deduplication process and a link to the unresolved contacts.

4

Please Stay in Touch

The crux of any good CRM is keeping track of our business interactions. You likely talk to your customers and prospects, email them, and have follow up items. In this chapter, we'll explore Activity management with Zoho CRM (Activity Types, Calendar preferences, time management) as well as tracking interactions.

Most calendaring software allows you to view your appointments and tasks, but there is no relationship between the activity and the person with whom or company with which it is scheduled. If you manage your schedule via a diary or a desk calendar, forgetting an appointment can be a problem. You have to flip through the pages until you find the name and/or appointment date. Likewise, you don't have a spot where you can easily see a list of all the appointments you've previously scheduled with the contact.

In Zoho CRM, you can associate Activities with just about any record type. Some interactions, like phone calls and email, can tie back to the appropriate records automatically.

In Zoho CRM there are three main Activity types:

- Calls
- Meetings
- Tasks

It's important to understand not only how to schedule these Activities, but where the scheduled items are viewed and how they are handled in Zoho CRM. For example, **Meetings** are "time-bound", and you would most likely schedule them through the calendars to make sure that you don't have a conflict for a specific time slot. **Tasks** are generally "status-bound" activities that don't have to be set for a specific time. **Calls** are a toss-up and can be scheduled as either a time-sensitive Call or a status-bound task.

Once the Activity occurs, you'll provide follow-up for completed activities using different methods. For example, most people assume that Meetings were held, so you do not need to "clear" them. On the other hand, a Task might only be partially completed, and you can mark a Task as "partially completed."

Activities play an important role in daily business operations, so you want to make sure you can access them easily. In Zoho CRM, your tasks are listed in three places:

- The user's **Homepage**
- The **Activities Module** page
- In the **Activities Related List** of any related records.

By default, your Tasks appear on your **Homepage**, but can be modified to include all your Activities. Zoho CRM's **Activities Module** gives you a listing of all the activities for all your contacts, leads, and accounts. The **Activities Module** is readily accessible by clicking Activities on the Zoho CRM Horizontal Navigation bar.

You can filter the Activities Module by using different criteria, such as the date range, type, priority, and the users whose activities you want to view. Try the Kanban view with your activities and you'll create a "whiteboard" for scheduling.

When creating an activity in Zoho CRM, you must enter Activity details such as Subject, Task Owner, Due Date, and the record to which the Task is related. You can also add custom fields to any of the Activity modules. For example, you might want to add a field to Meetings to indicate that it was a tradeshow or training activity, or add a field to the Tasks, to differentiate between sales and retention follow-ups.

In Zoho CRM, Activities are visible inside the record as a Related List. You can associate Activities with specific modules including Leads, Accounts, Contacts, Deals, and Campaigns.

Zoho CRM is Up to the Task

As mentioned earlier, Tasks are usually "status-bound" activities. Because they are not set for a specific time, they do not appear on your calendars. They appear on your Home page, in the Activities modules, and in the Related List area of any record with which the

Task is associated. It's very easy to create a Task in Zoho CRM. The hard part is actually completing the task! Here's all you need to get started:

1. Create a new Task. There are a few ways to schedule a new task depending on where you are in Zoho CRM:

    ✓ Click the **Plus** icon on the **Horizontal Navigation Bar** and choose **Task**.

    ✓ Go to the **Activities Module** and click the **Task** icon.

    ✓ Hover over the **Open Activities Related List** and click the **Plus Sign.**

    ✓ Access the **Open Activities Related List** on an individual record and click the **New Task** icon.

    As an example, let's say you're talking on the phone with a Contact; if you're on their record in Zoho CRM you can create the Task right from there. At other times, you might need generic reminders and schedule those from the Activities Module or the Horizontal Navigation Bar.

    All of these methods open the **Create Task** page.

2. Enter a **Subject** for the Task. This is the only required field. A good practice is to use the Subject as a brief description of what you need to do.

3. (Optional) Enter the additional Task details.

    ✓ **Due Date:** When this Task should be completed.

    ✓ **Priority:** Select Low, Normal or High.

    ✓ **Owner:** Feel free to pass the buck to one of your cohort.

    ✓ **Reminder:** Indicate if you want to receive a Reminder of your Activity via email, a popup in Zoho CRM, or both.

    ✓ **Repeat:** Schedule the Task to recur. This option does require you enter a Due Date.

4. (Optional) Click **More Fields**.

    ✓ **Contact:** The Contact for whom you are performing the Task.

Zoho CRM Essentials

- ✓ **Other Modules:** A Task can be related to an existing Deal, Case, Estimate, or Invoice.
- ✓ **Status:** Where you are in the process of completing the Task.
- ✓ **Description**: Expand on the subject of the task.

5. Click **Save**. The new Activity appears on your Home page Activity pane, the Activities Module, and in the Open Activities Related List area for the specified record.

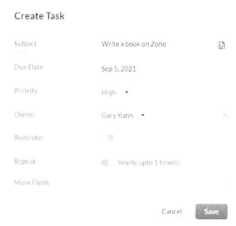

Fig 4-1 Create a Task

Customizing Tasks

Most Zoho CRM users are happy with the generic Zoho CRM Task format. However, some may want to take scheduling Tasks to the next level. For example, you might want to add in several standard subject lines for faster Task scheduling, or you may have your own Task Status verbiage. If you haven't already guessed, this can be easily done, but only by a Zoho Administrator.

1. Log into Zoho CRM as an Administrator.

2. Click the **Setup Gear** and then select **Modules and Fields** under the **Customization** header. The **Modules and Fields** page opens.

3. Click **Tasks** to open the **Tasks** page, and then **Standard** to open the **Layout Editor**. Modify the desired fields by clicking the **ellipsis** in the right-hand corner of the field.

4. Click **Edit Properties** to modify the pick list of each field.

Some common field modifications are:

- **Subject:** Indicates the main Task categories.
- **Priority:** Here's where you can change Low and High to "Meh" and "Do it or You're Fired", or to your company's preferred Priority rankings.
- **Status:** Modify this to include the typical milestones involved in completing your Tasks.

Clearing Tasks

As important as it is to create tasks, it is equally important to clear them. There are a couple of ways to complete or close a Task:

- From a List View in the Activities Module or the Open Activities Related List on a Record:
    - Hover over the Task.
    - Click the **Check** button.
- From within the Task page:
    - **Open** the **Task** that you want to close.
    - Click **Close Task.**

After you complete a task, Zoho CRM will:

- Stop reminding you about the activity
- Automatically update the **Closed Time** field
- Move the task from the Open Activities Related List to the Closed Activities Related List.

Not all Tasks are an open and shut case. If you change the Status of a Task to anything other than Completed, the Task remains open with your other Open Tasks.

Using the Zoho CRM Calendar for Scheduling a Meeting or Time Sensitive Calls

Meetings are time-sensitive activities that are conducted at a specific time, typically with a specific person, or related to a specific Account. Typical meetings include conference calls, seminars, and appointments.

The various Zoho CRM calendars are great for viewing and scheduling Meetings. You can schedule a Meeting the same way that you schedule Tasks and Calls. However, I recommend scheduling Meetings from a Calendar view. This way you can literally see if you have a conflict, or if you are open.

Here's how you schedule Meetings from the Calendar.

1. Click the **Calendar icon** on the far-right side of the **Zoho CRM Horizontal Navigation Bar**.
2. Select the **Day, Week or Month** view, depending on your personal calendar preference. The Calendar opens, displaying your scheduled Calls and Meetings.
3. (Optional) You can change the settings to display other users in your organization.
4. Click on the time slot that for the Meeting or Call; or, you can click the **Create** button.
5. If you are working from the Day or Week calendar, then clicking the time slot might make sense. If you are using the Month calendar, then the Create button might be easier.
6. Complete the Meeting screen with:

    ✓ Meeting **Name/Title**

    ✓ Indicate if the Meeting is an **online meeting**. If you are using Zoho Meetings for online meetings a meeting link is automatically created.

    ✓ (Optional) check **All Day** if the meeting should span the entire business day.

    ✓ Select the **From**, or start, date and time

    ✓ Select the **To**, or end, date and time

    ✓ Assign the **Host**. By default, this is **you**, but you can change the name to any other unsuspecting Zoho CRM user.

    ✓ (Optional) Add a **Participant(s).** You can add additional participants by clicking the Add link and searching for them. Participants receive an invitation to the Meeting.

    ✓ **Relate** the Meeting to a Record. Click the picklist

arrow to select the correct Module – Lead, Contact or Others (Accounts, Deals, etc.)
7. (Optional) Assign a **Repeat** option
8. (Optional) Select a **Participants Reminder** option.
9. Click **Add more details**. This is where you can add a detailed **Description** and set a reminder for yourself.
10. Click **Save** to save the Meeting. If you have a scheduling conflict, you receive a warning message; you can decide to proceed or change the time.

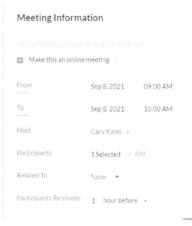

Fig 4-2 Creating a Meeting

If you added participants and they have an email address, you are asked if you want to send email invitations. Any Meetings scheduled this way appear in the Invited Meetings Related List and you are able to monitor their responses.

Sharing Your Calendar with Others

One of the great features of Zoho CRM is the ability to share your calendar with others. If you would like to take a peek at someone's calendar here's how:

1. Click the Calendar icon in the Horizontal Navigation Bar.
2. Select Users from the View Menu on the left side of the Calendar Navigation Bar.
3. Type in to find or scroll and select the name of the desired user(s).

Customizing the Calendar Preferences

Once you've started using the Zoho CRM calendar, you might want to tweak it a bit. For example, you might want to default all meetings to an hour, or eliminate Saturday and Sunday from the calendar altogether. You can easily customize your calendar experience.

To make changes to your Calendar settings:

1. Click **Options** on the **Calendar's Navigation Bar**
2. Click **Preferences**.

You can personalize preferences for:

- Days in week view: Select the days of the week do you want to display on your week view.
- Week starts on – select the day of the week to be the first on your calendar view.
- Day starts at – set the start of your typical work day.
- Day ends at – select the time to end your typical work day.
- Weekly Holiday 1 – indicate the first day of your "weekend" or non-workdays.
- Weekly Holiday 2 – select your second weekend or non-workday.
- Activity Type – Choose the Activity types to display on your Calendar.
    - ✓ Meetings
    - ✓ Calls
    - ✓ Appointments
- Default Meeting Duration
- Default Call Duration
- Hide meetings # days after they've ended
- Set when Meetings should drop off of your calendar view.
- Hide declined meetings
- Enable or Disable CalDAV (iPhone integration).The Preference settings are user specific, so they only apply to your calendar.

Please Stay in Touch

Fig 4-3 Customizing Calendar Preferences

I Want to Be Alone

Sometimes you may need to block out time on our calendar for an activity that isn't necessarily business related, but we need that time to show as unavailable. To schedule **Unavailable** time:

1. Click the time slot.
2. Choose **Mark As Unavailable.**
3. Enter the **From** (start date & time) and **To** (end date & time).
4. (Optional) **Enter Comments** – keep in mind, depending on your security settings, the comments are visible to other Zoho CRM users.

Avoid Senior Moments with a Note

Look around your desk. Do you have a legal pad filled with illegible scribbles? Look at your computer monitor; is it decorated with sticky notes?

Imagine that one of your more high-maintenance customers calls you on March 1 in immediate need of an imported, Italian widget. You check with your distributors and guarantee him one by March 15. On March 10, he calls you, totally irate that he hasn't yet received his widget.

Stop the insanity! You need to start taking advantage of Zoho CRM Notes!

Creating notes is one of the easiest features to master, but one that many users overlook. A simple note in Zoho CRM provides you with several benefits:

- ✓ Your entire office can operate smarter by being on the same page by having access to the same client data.
- ✓ You have a record or digital finger print, down to the date, time, and creator of all Notes entered for your Contacts.
- ✓ You won't forget important information.
- ✓ You have pertinent information at your fingertips without having to strip-search your office looking for a lost sticky note.

Considering the amount of power Notes hold, they are very simple to add.

1. **Navigate** to the **record** to which you want to add a Note.
2. Hover your cursor over **Notes** in the left-hand **Vertical Navigation Bar**
3. Click the **Plus** icon. The **Notes** window opens.
4. Fill in the **contents** of the note. Go ahead, write a book if you want.
5. (Optional) Add a **title** for the note. The note title will appear at the top of the note. If you add a lot of notes to a record, the subject makes it easier to scroll through and find one you want.

Please Stay in Touch

6. (Optional) Click the **Paperclip** icon to attach a file relevant to the Note

7. Click **Save** to save the note.

   The Note is saved and is listed with your three most recently created Notes. When creating a Note, you may notice that the date says simply Now. Don't worry; the date will appear the next day. By default, the person who creates the Note "owns" it, so you can easily figure out who noted what.

8. (Optional) Click **View Previous Notes** to see all of the Notes you added for a record.

Fig 4.4 Creating a Note

Once you create a Note or two, there is a bit more to the Notes than meets the eye. You can also:

- **See the complete date and time of the Note:** Hover your cursor over the **clock** at the bottom of the note.
- **View more information about the record:** Hover your cursor over the **record name** at the bottom of the note.
- **Delete a Note:** Hover your cursor to the right of the note and click the **Trash Can.**
- **Edit a Note:** Hover your cursor over the Note. Click the **Pencil** icon in the Contact Owner field, from the Contact Details page, and select another user.

You can also change the sort order of your Notes.

Emailing Your Contacts

A benefit of sending email from within Zoho CRM is that a history of the event is added to your contact's Closed Activity Related List. Since email is the primary form of business communication, having a record of all the emails sent to each of your contacts helps you keep track of it all. It also saves digging through your email client to find those conversations.

You can send emails to Contacts, Leads, and any other record on which you have an email address. Typically, you don't send email to Accounts as they don't have email addresses. When you compose an email, you can choose to send using any of the email accounts that you have configured. You can create your message from scratch using the email editor, or you can use a template.

There are a variety of ways to integrate email with Zoho CRM. You can integrate your existing email host, or you could migrate to Zoho Mail. Zoho Mail is Zoho's mail hosting service, which is offered at very competitive pricing.

Most Zoho CRM users continue to manage their day-to-day email sending and receiving, with an email client like Outlook or Gmail. Zoho CRM connects with most popular email clients including:

- GMail
- Office 365
- Zoho Mail
- Yahoo

To configure your email integration, click **Setup** then click the **Email** option in the **Channels** header. You also have a choice of POP/SMTP or IMAP connection types to connect to Zoho CRM. Without getting too technical, you should consider using IMAP. IMAP records both incoming and outgoing messages.

Be sure to have the following information handy before integrating your email:

- Incoming Mail Server name and port
- Outgoing Mail Server name and port
- Outgoing connection type
- Your name
- Your email user name
- Your email password

Zoho also knows users live in applications other than theirs. You can integrate Zoho CRM within many email clients via add-ins. For example, perhaps you spend most of your day in Outlook and prefer to manage your email there. No problem. Under Setup, explore the options for GMail and Microsoft. These add-ins enable access to Zoho CRM data work from within the email client. You can also synchronize your calendar and contacts with Zoho CRM.

Whew! That seems like a lot of information to process. Sending email is much easier.

1. Search for and click the record to email.
2. Click the **Send Email** button.
3. Click **Insert** to use a Template, add a Survey link, Forms Link, etc.
4. Enter a **Subject**.
5. Type your **email body**
6. (Optional) Click **Attach** to add an attachment.
7. (Optional) Click **Schedule** to send your email at a later time
8. Click **Send** to send, or Cancel if you changed your mind!

All email, both sent and received, appears on the Email Related List of the record. Zoho CRM provides the status of the sent emails, allowing you to see if the email was actually opened. And, as if that wasn't enough, you can click on an email subject line to open and see the full details of the email thread.

Want to delete an email from the Zoho CRM Closed Activities? Click the picklist at the top right of the emails section (by default, this says ALL). Select the filter – sent from CRM or IMAP, for instance. To delete the email:

1. Hover your cursor over the email
2. Click in the checkbox to select the email(s)
3. Click the Delete button

The email is deleted.

Pick Up the Phone and Dial

There is little doubt that you conduct a great deal of your business via email. However, you probably also make use of your phone; Zoho has a number of ways to make and log your phone calls.

Scheduling a Call

In Zoho CRM, Calls can be scheduled in two different ways:

> ➢ From the Calendar

➢ From a Record

Many Zoho users struggle when it comes to scheduling routine follow-ups. For example, you may want to phone every person you met at a recent trade show. A good rule of thumb would be to consider routine follow-ups as Tasks. Tasks are not time-sensitive and do not need to appear on your calendar. In fact, crowding dozens of follow-up calls on your calendar might make it hard for you to spot your important Meetings. Calls should be used for time sensitive activities such as conference calls that you want to appear on your calendar. You should also consider using some of the automated features of Zoho CRM to remind you about important follow-ups, rather than manually scheduling Calls for them.

Logging Calls

As mentioned earlier in this chapter, you can schedule Tasks and Calls to remind yourself of routine follow-ups. However, rather than scheduling these items manually, you might use another process. For example, you might take a look at your Home page every morning and call the people associated with Open Deals or New Leads.

Not scheduling a call in advance doesn't mean that you can't record a call history after the fact. Here's all you need to do:

1. Click **Calls** on the **Modules** bar.
2. Click **Create Call**.
3. Select Log a call. The **Log a Call** popup window opens.
4. Enter the appropriate information in the **Create Call** popup window.

   The only required information is the **Call Type** (Inbound, Outbound or Missed), the **Call Start Time,** and **Call Duration**. A call can be associated with both the Contact and their Account. Alternatively, a Deal, will be associated with the corresponding Contact.

5. Indicate the **Call Status** of Inbound, Outbound or Missed.
6. Click **Save** to log the call.

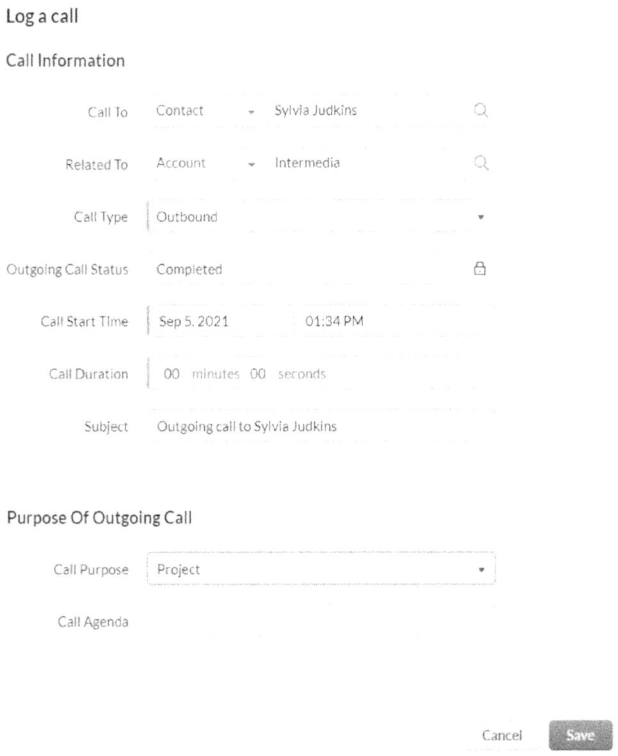

Log a call

Call Information

Call To	Contact ▾ Sylvia Judkins
Related To	Account ▾ Intermedia
Call Type	Outbound
Outgoing Call Status	Completed
Call Start Time	Sep 5, 2021 01:34 PM
Call Duration	00 minutes 00 seconds
Subject	Outgoing call to Sylvia Judkins

Purpose Of Outgoing Call

Call Purpose	Project
Call Agenda	

Cancel   **Save**

Fig 4.5 Logging a Call

Using a VOIP Phone Solution

If you are a salesperson, you likely depend on calls to communicate with prospects and customers. Remembering to record each and every call can be a daunting process. If you don't record those interactions, you can't measure the effectiveness of your calls, or even keep track of whom you've called. By integrating your phone system with Zoho CRM, you can make, receive, and record call histories, right from within Zoho CRM. You also have easy access to calls made, so you never lose track of previous conversations.

If you want to automate the phone calls, you will need to use a VoIP phone system that integrates with Zoho CRM. Be sure to research which phone system works the best for you. Not all systems offer the same functionality – or price! If you want more information, take a look at ***TechBenders.com/telephony*** where you can find a list of all the current telephony integration providers.

Most VoIP phone systems will include the capability to:

- ➢ Record calls from either your office or mobile phone
- ➢ Click to Dial
- ➢ Add notes to a call
- ➢ Automatically tie incoming calls to a record
- ➢ Create new records from incoming calls
- ➢ Call analytics

Once you choose your provider, it's fairly simple to setup it up in Zoho CRM.

1. Click **Settings.** The **Settings** page opens.
2. Choose **Telephony** in the Channels section.
3. Follow the prompts provided by your phone provider.

5

You Can Have It Your Way

I f you're the Database Administrator, you'll be responsible for setting up the database initially and making sure that your database purrs along in the future. As the Administrator you have access to the Setup module where you can perform great feats of daring, including creating fields, customizing layouts and managing system settings. You are also able to setup users, defining their access and permissions to specific Zoho areas and functions.

Setting up the System

If you're the Database Administrator, becoming familiar with the system configuration is a good practice. If you're the sole user of the database, these settings can save your sanity. If you share the database with other users, these settings can probably save you a lot of future head scratching.

To access Zoho CRM's Settings click the **Setup Gear** on far-right side of Zoho CRM's Horizontal Navigation Bar. The Settings page is divided into 10 areas; although I only cover the most basic ones, feel free to flip through the other settings.

Zoho CRM Essentials

Fig 5-1 The Setup Page

Before You Start Modifying Your Database

You're probably reading this book because you are relatively new to Zoho CRM. Unfortunately, there are a few mistakes that newbies very often make. Read on if you'd like to avoid making them!

Do Your Homework

Before getting started, I want to stress the importance of doing a bit of homework. I can't stress enough the importance of this step. Plan ahead - or you might end up with a big mess!

- ➢ Familiarize yourself with the existing Zoho CRM fields. All too often, new Zoho CRM users create a bevy of fields, only to discover down the road that a similar field already exists. For example, you don't need to create a Cell Phone Field if a Mobile Phone field already exists.
- ➢ Justify the need for the new field. Will it be used in a report? Do you need to segment or categorize your database by the field? If you can't justify it, don't create it!
- ➢ Determine what fields you're going to add and what type of data will be stored in those fields (dates, numbers, drop-down items). If the field is to contain a drop-down list, now is the time to compile that list!

Take the time to whiteboard, create a digital document or draw your database customization ideas and plan on a napkin. The key is: don't skip the planning. Whether going at the database design on your own or if you engage a Zoho Partner, it's important to map out your Zoho CRM customization prior to jumping in. It's always easier to do it right from the beginning than to try and fix the mess later!

To explore the Zoho CRM fields:

1. Click the **Setup Gear**. The **Setup** page opens.

2. Click **Modules and Fields** in the **Customization** area. You will be on the **Modules** tab.

3. Click the **Module** that you would like to analyze and then click the **Fields Tab**.

All of your fields are listed alphabetically by field name. Review this a bit to familiarize yourself with the "out of the box" fields before creating new ones.

Start by Creating the Lead Fields

I cannot stress this little tidbit of information enough. When you create a new Lead field, you are given the option to map it to the Contacts, Accounts and/or Deal modules. ***This option does not exist if a field is created in one of the other modules***. Upon Converting a Lead, Zoho CRM copies the Lead field data to the new module fields – Contacts, Accounts and Deals.

Most databases will carry over certain key pieces of information from one module to the next. For example, if you capture in a field the kind of boat motor a Lead has, chances are you need to see that information once the Lead is converted to an Account and/or Contact record. And you might want it to appear in Deal records as well. The choice is yours. Lead Conversion Mapping eliminates you having to retype those field values. You can either do something once, or you can do it four times. You be the judge!

Zoho CRM Essentials

Fig 5-2 Cloning a Lead Field to Account

You Can't Change the Field Type

Zoho CRM offers you a variety of different types of fields. Actually, 22 different field types are available, but who's counting? Make sure you get this right the first time. Zoho CRM does not allow you to simply change the field type later. You have to delete the field and then recreate it, using the correct field type. Remember the previous section when we suggested planning? Define in advance whether a field should be a **Pick List** which is based on a drop-down list, or a **Single Line** is a manually typed in character field.

Zoho CRM uses the following field type structure:

- ➤ **Single Line:** This is probably the most common of the field type choices; a Single Line field can contain both numbers and characters. The field holds a maximum of 255 characters.

- ➤ **Multi-Line:** This is where you can store a large amount of information that you don't want to risk burying away amidst your other notes. For example, you might want to include your driving directions in this area. This field can contain 65,000 characters.

- ➤ **Email**: It used to be that everyone you know had several phone numbers. Now, the chances are that your contacts have numerous email addresses. Here's your opportunity to include as many as you like.

- ➢ **Pick List:** If consistency is king, then this field type is the thing. Define a list of choices you and your users pick from to enter the field value. This ensures data consistency and standardization of field values.
- ➢ **Multi-Select:** This puppy is a pick-list based field. Similar to the Pick List type above, it's a great tool to ensure data consistency. And bonus, you can select multiple items when one choice simply isn't enough.
- ➢ **Phone**: This also enables dialing via telephony integration, if you have that configured.
- ➢ **Date**: When the time comes for you to enter information into a Date field, you see a tiny little calendar that enables you to select a date. The calendar supplies a useful purpose. If you create a field for an anniversary, like renewal or expiration date, and make it a character field, the other local yokels using the database might get creative and input anything from Jan 1 and January 1st to 01/01 and 1/1. Finding all renewal dates in the month of January would become an exercise in futility.
- ➢ **Date/Time**: When you want to be really exacting, create a Date/Time field to record the exact date and time of an event.
- ➢ **Number**: This field type enables you to enter only numbers. Say you want to find all your customers that have more than 30 employees. You can easily search for a number greater than 30, whereas you can't possibly search for a number greater than "thirty."
- ➢ **Auto-Number**: The field type allows you to specify the starting number in a sequence of numbers. And yes, you can add a Prefix as well. When creating new records, the auto-number field assigns the next value in the sequence.
- ➢ **Currency**: This field comes equipped with a dollar sign, appropriate commas, optional decimal places, and a sunroof (optional).
- ➢ **Percent**: A percent field is identical to a number field except it doesn't like commas. Or percent signs for that matter. Go figure!

- ➢ **Decimal**: This field accepts only numbers, a decimal point, and more numbers.
- ➢ **Long Integer**: Quite simply, this is a number field. Without a decimal point. Or a comma.
- ➢ **Check Box**: This actually creates a check box field that you can mark.
- ➢ **URL:** Use this field type if you need to associate another Web address with your contacts.
- ➢ **Lookup**: This field creates a "one-to-many" relationship. For example, it can be used to tie multiple tenants to the same apartment complex, or multiple Contacts to the same referral source.
- ➢ **Formula:** For those of us who might struggle with math, you can sit down, put your feet up and let Zoho CRM do the heavy lifting – as long as you were smart enough to figure out the correct equation in the first place!
- ➢ **User**: Similar to the Record Owner field, the User field type gives you a pick list of your current users. You have the option of limiting the field to allow for a single User selection or multiple. For example, you might need a field for Project Team or Project Lead. The Project Team might be one or a combination of your Zoho Users. The User field type offers the convenience of a picklist based on you Zoho Users.
- ➢ **File Upload**: This nifty keen field type allows you to upload a file, or up to 5 files (not exceeding 20 MB) from various locations including your local computer, Zoho WorkDrive, Zoho Docs, and Google Drive. This comes in handy when you need easy access to a service agreement or other pertinent document.
- ➢ **Image Upload**: Whether you need to store a picture of your client, a picture of their property or images of products they purchased, a picture is worth 1,000 words, and here's where you can upload up to 10 images (as long as they total less than 20 MB).
- ➢ **Multi-Select Lookup**: Zoho CRM elevates the one-to-many relationship by letting you create "many-to-many" relationships. As an example, you might have clients that attend many webinars and webinars with many attendees. Or a contractor that works with multiple clients and those clients work with multiple contractors.

Fig 5-3 Zoho Field Types

Changing the Existing Database Fields

A good place to start is by tweaking the existing fields. As you learned earlier, you can't change a field's type, but you can delete it or rename it. This is done by clicking the Ellipsis to the right of a field. Certain *core or system defined* fields - including Last Name and Lead Owner - are so important that Zoho CRM won't allow you to edit them.

Deleting a Field

If you delete a field from a database, all data in that field is deleted. Ironically, the monumental task of deleting a field is ridiculously easy to fulfill. To do so, just follow these steps:

1. Click the **Setup Gear**. The **Setup** page opens.

2. Click **Modules and Fields** in the **Customization** area. You will be on the **Modules Tab**.

3. Click the **Module** that you would like to change and then click the **Standard Layout**. For now, we are going to concentrate on the main layout; later you can add additional layouts.

4. (Optional) Remove any unwanted fields by clicking the Ellipsis that appears after the field and choosing **Remove Field**. The deleted field will move to the ***Unused Fields*** area on the left of the screen. The Unused Fields area works like a Recycle Bin. When you are positive you no longer want the field – and all of its data – you can remove the field permanently by clicking the Trash Can icon.

Renaming a Field

Another quick database customization is to rename one of the existing fields to make it more in tune with your own lexicon. For example, you might be old school and want to change **Mobile** to **Cell**.

Adding a New Field

Believe it or not, your homework is the hard part. Once you're done with that, adding your custom fields is easy. Just remember that only Zoho CRM users with the Modules Customization permission can modify the database structure.

Make sure to start by adding your Leads module fields first. This is the only time you are asked if you would also like to add corresponding fields to the Account, Contact and/or Delete Deal modules. It can be done manually later, but customizing the Leads Module first makes quick work of adding your custom fields to related modules.

The actual addition of fields is relatively easy. Drag a field type to your layout, tweak it a bit and voilà! You're done. Okay, there are actually a few steps involved but you get what I mean:

1. Click the **Setup Gear**. The **Setup** page opens.

2. Click **Modules and Fields** under the **Customization** header. You will be on the **Modules Tab**.

3. Click the **Module** that you would like to edit and then click the **Standard** layout.

4. From the **New Fields** tool pallet, select the field type and drag the **Field Box** to the desired location of your layout.

5. Enter a **name** for your new field

6. To edit the properties of the field, click the **Ellipsis** at the end of the new field and select **Edit Properties**. Depending on the field type you have a number of choices here including:

- ✓ **Field Label**: Edit the name of the field.
- ✓ **Number of characters allowed:** Standard fields can contain up to 255 characters. Multi-line fields can contain anywhere from 2,000 to 32,000 characters.
- ✓ **Required:** To make the field mandatory, place a check mark here.
- ✓ **Do not allow duplicate values:** This field type helps reduce the creation of duplicate records. When you enable this option, a new record can't be created with the same value in this field. You can have up to 2 unique fields per module. A good example of a "Do not allow duplicate values" field is Email Address.
- ✓ **Encrypt field:** Field data is stored in an encrypted, secure format.
- ✓ **Show Tooltip:** Think of this as training wheels for your field. As an example, you might add a Tooltip to the City field reminding your users not to use abbreviations.
- ✓ **Also create for:** If you are creating a new field in the Leads module this is your one and only time to replicate the field in the Account, Contact or Deal module. Otherwise, you'll have to create fields in the related modules manually.

7. (Optional) Click the **Ellipsis** at the end of the new field and select **Mark as required**. This makes another opportunity to make the field required.

8. (Optional) from the **Ellipsis**, click **Set Permission**. Set the access to fields by User Profiles to either *Read and Write* access to the field, *Read Only* access, or **Don't Show**.

9. (Optional) Click the **Preview** link to get a peek at what your final Layout will look like. If you set Profile based permissions, select the Profile from the picklist to view the Layout as that user Profile. Click the **X** when you are finished with your preview.

10. Click **Save** or **Save and Close** when you are finished creating fields.

It's easy to identify all the fields that you've create; all the user-created field labels are brown and all of the Zoho CRM "out of the box fields" are black.

Picking from Pick Lists

A sure-fire way to destroy a database's integrity is adding inconsistent data. Pick Lists or **drop-down** list-based fields ensure that users input uniform data. To edit a Pick List field:

1. Click the **Setup Gear**. The **Setup** page opens.

2. Click **Modules and Fields** under the **Customization** header. You will be on the **Modules Tab**.

3. Click the **Module** to customize and then click the **Standard** layout. The **Standard Layout** page for your module opens.

4. Click the **Ellipsis** button to the right of any of your **Pick List** fields and select **Edit Properties**. The **Pick List** fields are easy to identify as you will see **Option 1** in the middle of the field.

5. Newly added Pick List fields have two default values, Option 1 and Option 2. Click the Pick List item to edit the **Pick List** options.

6. (Optional) Scroll through the **Pick List Options**, hover your mouse over an item and click the minus button to remove it. The value is sent to the **Unused Values** list.

7. (Optional) Click and drag the value up or down to **reorder** the **Pick List**.

8. Click **Done** to save your changes.

You Can Have It Your Way

Fig 5-4 Creating a Pick List

Adding Pick List Options

From time to time, you may need to add additional options to your Pick Lists. There are a couple ways to do this. The first is great when you need to add one or two options:

1. Click the **Ellipsis** button on the **Pick List** field from the **Layout Editor**

2. Select **Edit Properties**.

3. Hover your mouse over the right-side boarder and click the **Plus** icon to add a new option.

4. (Optional) Scroll through the **Pick List Options**, hover your mouse over an item you wish to delete and click the minus button to remove it. The field will be sent to the **Pick List Recycle Bin**. If this is a brand-new **Pick List** you will want to delete Option 1 and Option 2.

5. (Optional) Grab any field by the left-side boarder and drag it up or down to reorder the Pick List.

6. Click **Done** when complete.

Adding Pick List Options in Bulk

Zoho CRM is designed to save you time whenever possible. And let's face it: customizing a new database can take up a lot of time. Although adding pick list items isn't difficult it can be time consuming, especially if you already have a list of the pick list items. As an example, you might have an existing list of the NAIC codes you want added to your database, or the counties in a state.

To import your pick list items:

1. Click the **Ellipsis** button on **Pick List** field and select **Edit Properties**. The Pick List popup opens.

2. Click the **Add Options in Bulk** link.

3. (Optional) Click **From Predefined Choices** to save yourself some typing. This option offers common pick lists like days of the Week and Months of the year.

4. (Optional) Click **From Unused Values** to use add back previously deleted options.

5. (Optional) Click **Manual Entry** to paste a list of items you copy from another source, like a list in a document or spreadsheet. Alternatively, you can manually type the options, tapping the Enter key between each option.

6. Click **Add Choices** when finished.

Other Pick List Options

There are a few more Pick List options that you might want to include in your database. Remember, the more restrictions you place on your data the more consistent it will be.

1. Click the **Ellipsis** button on the **Pick List** field from the **Layout Editor**

2. Select **Edit Properties**.

3. Select the following options as necessary:

    ✓ **Select default value:** If you have a frequently used value for the field, set that option as a default value. For example, if most of your business is in the United States you can select United States as the default value for the Country field.

- ✓ **Enable history tracking:** If the value in the Pick List field should be a progression over time, you may want to record a history of that life cycle as it changes. For instance, you may want a history of when the Lead Status changes from Attempted to Contact to Contacted.

- ✓ **Display values alphabetically:** Check this box to automatically reorder your Pick List in alphabetical order.

- ✓ **Required:** This option makes the Pick List field mandatory.

- ✓ **Show Tooltip:** Tick this box to display a hint or bread crumb for the user when they hover over the field.

Securing Access to Fields

Field level security is an issue for any organization that has multiple database users. There are many reasons why you may want to limit access to the various fields. First, you might secure a field to avoid a user accidentally changing a key piece of information, such as an account number. Secondly, you might want to limit the information that a user sees.

A credit card number is a great example of a field that you might want to secure. The bookkeeper might have full access to the field, because he or she needs the ability to add or change credit card numbers. The order takers might need to see the numbers, but not change them. Finally, the fulfillment center might not need access those numbers at all. In fact, management would probably rest easier knowing that only a select few have access to those numbers.

It's easy enough to change the field level security on a field-by-field basis. However, you may lose track of which fields you previously locked down over time, or you may wish to change the settings for multiple fields at one time.

1. Click the **Setup Gear**. The **Setup** page opens.

2. Click **Modules and Fields** under the **Customization** header. You will be on the **Modules Tab**.

3. Click the **Module** that you would like to change and then click the **Fields** tab.

4. Click the **Field Permissions** button. By default, Field Listing is selected.

   Your Fields are listed in alphabetical order with their field permissions displayed as columns.

5. Select a **Profile** from the drop-down. Do not assume that an Administrator should have access to all fields. For example, you may have designated your IT staff as Administrators, but this doesn't necessarily mean they should have the keys to the castle – or access to all the credit card information.

6. Select a Permission for each field. You have a total of three choices:

   ✓ **Read and Write**: Users can see and modify the data in a field.

   ✓ **Read Only:** Users can see the data in a field, but they can't change it.

   ✓ **Don't Show:** Users can neither see nor modify the data in a field.

7. Click **Save** to save your selections.

Fig 5-5 Changing Field Permission

Manufacturing Custom Modules

Just as you can add and customize fields to your database, you can also add custom Modules. Using Modules is a great way to add flexibility to your database. Once created, a Module appears on the Zoho CRM main menu, and you can view a list of all the records in the new module.

An example of when a custom Module might be a good idea is an Equipment module that lists the various pieces of Equipment associated to a customer. You may track the serial number, warranty info and make and model of the equipment. That is then associated to the Accounts or Contacts record(s) that purchased that specific item. Realtors may want a module for the properties they are working with. Recruiters might have a module for each job opening that they are looking to fill. The possibilities are endless!

Renaming a Module

The modules in a standard Zoho CRM database come pre-named. Those module names may not match your existing business language. Change is hard and you might find it challenging to change the terminology that you've been using for years.

Depending on your industry, you might deal with "students" or "candidates" rather than Contacts and you might need to see a list of your "hospitals" or "families" rather than Accounts. You can simply rename the existing modules to better fit your vernacular. Changing a module name can only be done by a database Administrator.

There are a few Modules that cannot be renamed. For example, you can rename the Quotes tab to "Estimates", but you cannot rename the Reports or Dashboard tabs.

To rename a Module:

1. Click the **Setup Gear**. The **Setup** page opens.

2. Click **Modules and Fields** under the **Customization** section. You will be on the **Modules** Tab.

3. Hover your mouse over the Module that you would like to change, and click **Rename**.

4. Enter a plural and singular form of the new Module name. For example, one record might be referred to as a Suspect but many records would be considered Suspects.

5. Click **Save**.

Sharing a Module with Other Users

As you add Zoho CRM users, you might find that those users are not seeing the same information. By default, Zoho CRM modules are not shared and users can only view the records they created, or records to which they are assigned the **Record Owner**. To change this, you can change the access to your modules. Prior to doing this, you should first configure a hierarchy of access by configuring Profiles. It is much easier to change an individual user's Profile than it is to change the access for multiple fields and Contacts.

1. Click the **Setup Gear**. The **Setup** page opens.
2. Click **Modules and Fields** in the **Customization** area. You will be on the **Modules** Tab.
3. Hover your mouse over the Module that you would like to change, and then click **Module Permission**.
4. Select the **Profile**(s) to which to grant access to that Module.
5. Click **Save** to save your changes.

Creating a Custom Module

Like a family tree, a module can have multiple relationships with other modules. For example, the Accounts module is related to the Contacts, Leads, and Deals modules. After you establish a relationship between modules, the related modules appears as a **Related List** in a record's Detail view. In the example of the Accounts module, Contacts, Leads, and Deals appear as Related Lists in an Account's Detail view because they are *related* to the Accounts module.

When you create a Module, you need to specify its relationship to other modules. A new module can have multiple relationships with other modules. You specify these relationships through the use of **Lookup fields**.

1. Click the **Setup Gear**. The **Setup** page opens.
2. Click **Modules and Fields** in under the **Customization** area. You will be on the **Modules Tab**.
3. Click the **New Module** button. The new module's **Edit** page opens.

4. Enter a Module name in the top left corner of the **Edit** page, unless you would like the module to be call "Untitled."

5. Customize the Module by dragging fields to the Layout.

6. By now you should be an old hand at this. Drag the fields around the layout as you create your masterpiece. However, because the new Module will be related to one or more of the existing Modules you need to add at least one **Lookup Field**:

    ✓ **Lookup**: This field relates a single record in the new module to another record in another module. For example, if you created a new module to track serial numbers, each serial number would be unique to one Contact record.

    ✓ **Multi-Select Lookup**: This field allows you to relate the new module to multiple contacts in another module. For example, if the new module is to track properties then you would probably want to associate many records with the property and the property to many other records. This is the definition of a many-to-many relationship.

7. Click **Save** to save the new module.

Deleting a Custom Module

You can delete a module and send it to the Recycle Bin if you feel that it is just not working in the way you had envisioned. Just remember that any information you entered into the custom module will be deleted as well.

1. Click the **Setup Gear**. The **Setup** page opens.

2. Click **Modules and Fields** under the **Customization** header. You will be on the **Modules Tab**.

3. Hover your mouse over the **Module** that you would like to delete and select **Delete**.

4. Click **OK** to confirm the deletion.

Working with Subforms

A Subform is a secondary form that lets you add multiple line items to your primary form. You can use Subforms to track credit card information, previous employment records or emergency contacts. You have a main contact, A **Subform** allows you to store all the pertinent information about a record so you don't have to go on a wild goose chase hunting down related information.

Not sure whether you should be using a custom Module or a Subform? Consider how you'll use the secondary data. When you create a new module, you can:

- Add records that are independent of other records.
- Access a list of all Module records.
- Perform lookups or queries to find and filter the records.
- Report on the records independent of other modules.

For example, you might manufacture various products that aren't initially associated with a contact record. Additionally, you would like to be able to access a list of all your products to determine which one has been associated with a contact and which one is still available to sell. If that's the case, a custom Module would be your best bet.

Subforms do not exist outside of the record with which they are associated. In the case of Mr. Big, you do not need to access this information unless you are working directly with Mr. Big.

To create a Subform:

1. Click the **Setup Gear**. The **Setup** page opens.
2. Click **Modules and Fields** under the **Customization** area. You will be on the **Modules Tab**.
3. Click the **Module** that you would like to edit and then click **Standard Layout**. The **Standard Layout** page for your module opens.
4. Drag the **Subform** field to the appropriate area of your layout from the New Fields tool pallet.
5. Click the **Add Field** hyperlink. You will see a very familiar list of field types.
6. Click a field type to add it to the Subform.
7. Enter a field name.
8. Repeat Steps 5 – 7 above as needed.

9. (Optional) Rearrange the fields dragging it to the desired location.

10. Click **Save** to save your Subform.

Fig 5-6 Creating a Subform

Working with Layouts

A *Layout* is how you actually see the fields in your database. Think about how you want your fields arranged on your Layout. For example, you may want the main business phone number on the top portion of your layout, and address information on the bottom.

Creating a Section in Your Layout

You might prefer to create a **Section** for fields that belong together; for example, you might have a section for address information and another one for phone numbers. Here's what you need to know:

1. Click the **Setup Gear**. The **Setup** page opens.

2. Click Modules and Fields in the Customization area. You will be on the **Modules Tab**.

3. Click the **Module** that you would like to change and then click the **Standard** layout.

4. Drag the **New Section** from the **New Fields** area to the desired location on your layout.

5. Give the **New Section** a new moniker.

6. Drag fields from other sections to the new section or drag new fields from the **New Fields tool pallet** to the **Section**.

7. (Optional) Click the section's **Gear Icon**. You have two choices here:

    ✓ **Section Layout:** Choose either **Single Column** or **Double** Column to display your fields in one or two columns.

✓ **Tab Order:** Choose either **Left to Right** or **Top to Bottom** to determine how your cursor moves when you tap the Tab key to move from field to field.

8. Click **Save** to save your changes.

Speed It Up with Quick Create Layouts

Zoho CRM Lookup fields are extremely powerful in that they help you to relate two records together. For example, you might want to relate a new Contact to one of your existing Vendors. But what happens if you want to relate a new Contact to a Vendor that is not already in your database? Theoretically you could first create the new Vendor, create the new Contact and then link them together. However, there's a neat Zoho CRM trick called the ***Quick Create*** layout.

The Quick Create layout is a mini layout that you can use to create a new record when entering data in a lookup field. The Quick Create layout is layout-specific, or parent Layout. You can create different Quick Create layouts for each of your existing layouts. If you work with multiple layouts, Zoho CRM prompts you to select the **Quick Create** layout as you create the new linked record.

1. Click the **Setup Gear**. The **Setup** page opens.

2. Click **Modules and Fields** under the **Customization** header. You will be on the **Modules** tab.

3. Click the **Module** that you would like to change and then click the **Standard Layout**. The **Standard Layout** page for your module opens.

4. Click the **Quick Create** Tab at the top of the Layout view. The **Quick Create** page opens.

5. Drag the desired fields from the **Available Fields** area on to the **Quick Create Layout**. Remember, this is supposed to make entering the new record as quick as possible, so you might want to limit yourself to a half dozen fields.

6. Click **Save** to save your **Quick Create** layout. You do not have to name the new Quick Create layout. It is given the same name as the parent layout to which it is associated.

You Can Have It Your Way

Fig 5-7 Quick Create Layout

Using the Detail View

A fresh Zoho CRM database includes a lot of related Modules that your organization, depending on your industry, may or may not need. The **Detail View** allows you to customize which related lists are displayed and how they are organized on the record Detail View. You can also customize and rearrange the columns in the related list sections. The Detail View also allows you to customize the **Business Card** section, which is the section that appears at the top of a record.

To edit the **Detail View**:

1. Click the **Setup Gear**. The **Setup** page opens.

2. Click **Modules and Fields** under the **Customization** header. You will be on the Modules Tab.

3. Click the **Module** that you would like to change and then click **Standard layout**. The **Standard Layout** page for your module opens.

4. Click the **Detail View** Tab. The Detail View page opens.

5. The first section is the **Business Card**. The Business card slider appears green if it is enabled. Disable this section by clicking the slider.

Editing the Business Card

If you have a lot of fields in your database, finding a specific field might involve some scrolling. The Business Card is a small section at the top of the record detail. It's a great way to keep the key fields handy and at virtual eye level. The Business Card is module specific, and global to all users. Meaning, how you customize this area is how it is displayed for all users. The number of fields is limited by module and is typically no more than 5 fields. To customize the Business Card:

1. Click **Customize** from the **Detail View**. A popup window opens with a list of that module's fields.

2. Click the **check mark** next to the fields to display in the **Business Card**. Remember, you're likely limited to no more than 5 fields.

3. (Optional) Hover your mouse on the **right-edge** of any of the selected fields to drag it up or down.

4. Click **Done** to save your changes to the Business Card, and then **Save** to save these changes to your layout.

The fields you selected for the Detail View will now appear at the top of your layout when you view a contact.

Editing the Related Lists

Under the Business Card section there are several default ***Related Lists***. You may not need all of the default related lists. For example, you may not want to add attachments to your database and therefore you don't need the Attachments related list.

To edit your Related Lists:

1. Scroll down to the Related List section to edit and click **Customize.**

2. Select or deselect the column headings to display in the Related List

3. (Optional) Drag the column headings up or down to rearrange their display order

4. Click **Save.**

5. Repeat steps 1 – 4 for the remaining Related Lists.

6. Click **Save** or **Save and Close** when complete.

Remember, less is more here. Select the most important columns to display. If you select too many columns, the Related List section may get crowded, causing unnecessary scrolling.

Add a New Layout

In Zoho CRM, you can create multiple Layouts per module. There are a few scenarios where this is useful. One is that you want to assign a specific Layout to specific user profiles. The other is you have different types of records within a module that have very different data fields associated with it.

In the user **Profile** scenario, this extends Zoho CRM's functionality by:

> ➢ Limiting the fields that a user can see based on their profile.
>
> ➢ Limiting the drop-down choices that a user can access.

As an example, your database might be shared by your customer service and sales departments. There might be certain fields, such as name, address, and phone numbers, that are required for both departments. However, there might be a few "department-specific" fields that only need to be accessed by a specific team. In addition, each department may only need to access certain drop-down items. For example, the follow up process for each department might be totally different.

Another reason to use different layouts would be if you have two very separate facets to your business. For example, let's say you sell cars and motorcycles. Cars might have one very specific set of fields while motorcycles have a very different array of fields. With separate Layouts, you can create separate input interfaces for the different records.

To create a new Layout:

1. Click the **Setup Gear.** The **Setup** page opens.

2. Click **Modules and Fields** under the **Customization** header. You will be on the **Modules Tab.**

3. Click the **Module** to which you would like to add an additional layout. The **Module Layout** page opens.

4. Click the **New Layout** button.

5. Add or delete fields and sections to the Layout as required.

6. (Optional) Edit any of the Pick List fields. Remember, pick list choices are specific to the Layout.

7. Click **Save** when you are finished creating the new layout. The **Layout Permissions** popup window appears.

8. Enter the Profiles that should have access to the new Layout.

9. Click **Save** to save your changes.

After you have created the new layout, users with permissions to multiple layouts can choose the appropriate layout when they add or edit records.

Mapping Lead Fields for Conversion

Few people enjoy wasting time, and duplicate entry can be a huge time waster! If you create a cohesive Lead Conversion Map, the Contact, Account and/or Deal fields automatically populate with the information from the original Leads field when you convert the Lead.

To map the fields for Lead Conversion:

1. Click the **Setup Gear.** The **Setup** page opens.

2. Click **Modules and Fields** under the **Customization** header. You will be on the **Modules** Tab.

3. Hover your mouse over the **Leads Module** and then click **Lead Conversion Mapping**. The **Conversion Mapping** page opens displaying the fields of the Standard layout of Leads, Contacts, Accounts and Deals.

4. **Map** the corresponding field for the Contacts, Accounts, and/or Deals by selecting the corresponding Lead field from the dropdown list. If no mapping is required select **None**. Notice that your custom fields are denoted with an asterisk.

5. Click **Save** to save your changes.

Fig 5-8 Conversion Mapping

6

Batten Down the Hatches

It can take a long time to develop a database. Unfortunately, it can take someone only a matter of moments to destroy it. Fortunately for you, there are a number of things that the database administrator(s) can do to protect your data.

Managing Database Users

A *User* is a person who logs into your database. Typically, each unique person accessing your database should have a User account. If several people enter data into your Zoho CRM database, I highly recommend setting up each person as a separate User. If you and Jane are both setup as Users of the database, make sure that you log in as you and Jane logs in as herself. Zoho CRM automatically captures several key pieces of information based on the logged in User. For example, you're assigned as the record creator of each new record that you add. Meetings, Calls or Tasks are also assigned and tracked by User. Having unique, identifiable Users in a database allows you to view your own activities on a calendar. Otherwise, you might find yourself driving to Podunk to visit Jane's mom on her birthday!

In Zoho CRM, a User is somebody who manages records, whether their own or those shared by other Users. In addition to accessing data, some of the Users can be designated as *Administrator Users*; they can perform administrative functions for the entire CRM account. Administrators can add Users to Zoho CRM.

In Zoho CRM the number of Users you can add is equal to the number of licenses you pay for. When you delete a User, the license is still active. You can either add another User to replace the deleted User, or you can cancel the license with Zoho CRM.

One lucky User is the **Super Admin**. He's the guy who setups up the billing information and adds new Users to Zoho CRM. He's the guy you have to bribe to help you with login issues. There can only be one Super Admin in Zoho, but you can have as many Admin Users as necessary.

Once you've added Users to Zoho CRM, get ready to rumble! The purpose of the game is to decide exactly what each User can do and access within Zoho CRM. Zoho CRM has two main ways of managing database permissions and access:

> **Profile**: This defines the features and Module permissions.
>
> **Role**: This defines the *data* that a User can access.

The best practice is to setup the Profiles and Roles prior to adding Zoho CRM Users, because the Profile and Role are assigned to new Users when you create them.

Profiling Your Users

In Zoho CRM a User Profile determines what you can and cannot do. This Profile covers any and all Modules of Zoho CRM. All Users with the same Profile have the same permissions which are generally the ability to View, Create, Edit and/or Delete records and manage Zoho CRM features such as importing and exporting data.

Profiles do not determine what records you can access; they determine what you can do with the records to which you have access.

Out of the box Zoho CRM comes with two profiles:

> Administrators: This Profile has access to all features and Modules. There must be at least one database Administrator.
>
> Standard Users: This profile has limited access to Zoho CRM administrative features and can access all Modules.

If the default Profiles don't quite cover your needs, you can create a new, custom profile:

1. Click the **Setup Gear**. The **Setup** page opens.
2. Click **Security Control** in the **Users and Control** area. You will be on the Profiles Tab of the Security Control page.

3. Click on the **New Profile** button. The **Create New Profile** popup window opens.

4. Enter the new **Profile Name**.

5. Choose an existing Profile to clone. If the new Profile should have most privileges, start with Administrator. Clone Standard if they are going to be more restricted.

6. (Optional) Specify a **Profile Description** and then click **Create**.

   You might think you're finished at this juncture; actually, your work is just beginning if you take a look at the profile page that opens. The only thing that might seem missing is a Save button; your changes will be saved automatically as you make them. You'll notice that the permissions are grouped into four categories

   ✓ **Basic permissions** - These permissions apply to the CRM modules and how Users can interact with those modules.

   ✓ **Setup Permissions:** This controls who is able to perform a variety of setup functions including managing Users, customizing modules and managing automations. You can mass enable or disable Setup permission by clicking the Setup Permissions button at the top of the section.

   ✓ **Extension Permissions:** This permission applies to anyone who will be integrating your Zoho account other Zoho apps.

   ✓ **Developer Permissions**: Like the title implies, these permissions would only be needed by a developer.

7. Scroll down the list and turn permissions on or off as necessary.

Zoho CRM Essentials

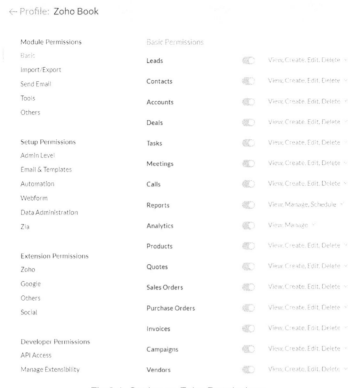

Fig 6-1. Setting up Zoho Permissions

Doing the Rock 'N Role

Roles **allow you to define how you share CRM data among Users based on your company's hierarchy.** Roles are assigned when you create the User. Roles determine which records a User can access. Roles do not determine the features and functionality the Users have within modules; that is the function of a Profile.

As an example, you may decide that your sales people should only see their own records. An administrator, by default, has permission to access all records.

Out of the box Zoho CRM has two Roles:

- CEO
- Manager

Because the Users with the role of CEO are higher up on the hierarchy, they can see all the contacts that are added by the Manager. However, the Managers only see their own Contacts, by default. Managers cannot see Contacts added by a CEO role User.

When you add a new Role, you decide where in the hierarchy those Users fall. Based on the hierarchy created, Users can only see the data of Roles below them on the hierarchy.

Roles can share data with other Users on their branch of the hierarchy with the Share Data with Peers option.

Whew! This can get a bit overwhelming! To sum up the rules of engagement:

- Users with the CEO role have access to the entire database.
- Managers cannot view or edit their subordinates' records if they do not have the "Read" or "Edit" permissions for the module.
- Users at a higher role can access other Users' data below their hierarchy. For example, a Sales Manager can access his/her subordinates' data.
- By default, Users of the same role cannot access each other's data. However, you can enable sharing of data among Users of the same role using the **Share Data with Peers** option when defining Roles.
- Access to a record applies to all functionality associated with that record. For example, you won't be able to add notes, schedule an appointment or create a deal for a contact if you don't have access to the record.

Although the concept might seem complex; creating roles is very easy:

1. Click the **Setup Gear**.
2. Click **Security Control** in the **Users and Control** area.
3. Click the **Roles** tab.
4. Click the **New Role** button.
5. Add the following information in the **New Role** page:
   - ✓ Enter the **Role Name**.
   - ✓ Select the immediate superior's Role from the

> **Reports To** lookup. If you do not select the superior's role, the new Role is created under the CEO Role.
>
> ✓ Select the **Share Data with Peers** to enable access rights other Users with the same Role.

6. (Optional) Specify the **Description** for the role.

7. Click **Save** to save the new role.

Getting Territorial about your Contacts

Segregating access to Contacts by role works well for most companies. You might want to think of the Role's hierarchy as an inverted triangle; those at the top have access to the most contacts while those lower down in the food chain have access to fewer contacts. However, this hierarchy falls apart for two basic reasons:

- ➤ Users can be assigned to only one role.
- ➤ The hierarchy is based on record ownership.

Take the example of a typical sales department with three roles: Admin, Manager and Sales. The Managers can see all the contacts added by the Sales Departments, and the Admins can see all the contacts added by both the Managers and the Sales people. But what happens if the sales people need to access certain vendors or shared accounts that have been added by the Admins or Managers? This becomes a job for the *Territories* feature.

Use Territories if you want to limit access to records based on criteria including geography, industry, or product interest. For example, you might create Territories for the Northeast and Southeast, or for access to vendors and resellers.

There are two ways to manage territories:

- ➤ **Automatically:** Territories are automatically assigned to Accounts, related Contacts and Deals when they are created or modified. Admins and Territory Managers cannot remove or modify record territories.

- ➤ **Manually:** Admins and Territory Managers can manually assign records to Territories. They can also remove or change Territories for any record.

The first step in the process is to turn on the territory feature:

1. Click the **Setup Gear**. The **Setup** page opens.

2. Click Territory Management in the **Users and Control** area. You will be on the Territory Management page.

3. Click the **Get Started** button.

4. Click the **Start from Scratch** option.

   This option makes a bit more sense than the **Extend from Role Hierarchy** option as the entire purpose of Territories is to be able to define data access beyond the Role structure. Territories manage data from the Lead or Account level and then that is passed to the Contacts that belong to the Accounts.

5. Click Create New Territory.

6. (Optional) If this is the first time you've wandered into Territories click the **I Understand. Enable Now** button.

   At this point you've created the top of the hierarchy.

7. Click the **New Territory** button. If you feel a sense of **Deja Vue** don't worry; you're right! However, this time the **Create Territory** page should open.

8. Specify the following options in the **Create Territory** page:

   - ✓ **Name**
   - ✓ **Territory Manager**: Pick the head honcho from your list of Users.
   - ✓ **Parent Territory:** This is how you start building your hierarchy.
   - ✓ **Users:** As the name implies, this is where you assign your database Users to the territory.
   - ✓ **Permissions:** You can assign Read Only or Read/Write/Delete permissions to the Users.
   - ✓ **Account Rule:** Specify the criteria for the records. Based on this rule criteria, Territories are assigned to Leads or Accounts.

9. Click **Create** to save your territory.

Zoho CRM Essentials

Fig 6-2 Creating Terriories

Adding a New User to the Mix

Once the Roles and Profiles are setup, adding a User is relatively easy. The number of Users you can add is based on your Zoho CRM edition and the number of User licenses purchased.

Each User signs in with an email address and password. Every User is given a Role and Profile. Remember, the Profile determines what features a User can perform and the Role determines what data the User can access.

If you've been following along at home, you created Roles and Profiles that enable the Users to carry out their day-to-day business and leave you with the security of knowing that they can't abscond with the entirety of your database should they decide to seek employment elsewhere. Your next step is to tie everything together.

1. Click the **Setup Gear**. The **Setup** page opens.

2. Click **Users** in the **Users and Control** area. You will be on the Users Tab of the **Users and Control** page.

3. Click the **Add New User** button. The **Assign CRM to User(s)** window opens.

4. Enter the following details:

- ✓ **First Name & Last Name:** Only the last Last Name is required.
- ✓ **Email:** Enter the User's valid email address. An invitation is sent to this email address.
- ✓ **Role:** Assign the Role of the User in your organization.
- ✓ **Profile:** Choose a Profile that defines the User's access rights in your Zoho CRM account.
- ✓ **(Optional) Territory**: Assign a Territory for the User. This option is available only if you have enabled Territories.

5. Click **Save** to save your changes.

Zoho sends an invitation to the User's email address that includes a link to Zoho CRM. The User has seven days to respond to the email. If they don't respond, the Administrator can resend the email invitation and the User risks the chance of being publicly humiliated at the next office meeting. Once the User confirms the email, they are active.

The Users can add their details like their phone numbers, address, and a profile picture. The User is also responsible for creating their own password. To edit the Zoho CRM account info, click the silhouette icon in the top right corner of Zoho CRM. The user can update their User record details by:

1. Click the **Settings** gear icon.
2. Under the **General Settings** header, click **Personal Settings**.
3. Click the **Edit** icon next to the **Username**.
4. **Update** and/or enter the details.
5. Click **Save**.

Validation Rules to Ensure Accuracy

One of the most challenging tasks in any CRM system is ensuring the validity of data. A poorly maintained database can cost a company in more ways than one: inaccurate reports, unreliable queries and marketing efforts and the constantly cleaning up and correcting of errors.

Validation Rules allow you to define the accuracy and validity of your data. If a field value entered for a record does not fulfill the Validation Rule, you receive an alert and you cannot save the record. When defining the Validation Rule, you can choose to have an alert when a specific condition is or is not met.

Here's how to create a Validation Rule:

1. Click the **Setup Gear**. The **Setup** page opens.
2. Click **Modules and Fields** in the **Customization** area. You will be on the **Modules Tab** of the **Modules and Fields** page.
3. Select the **Module** for which you want to create the Validation Rule.
4. Click the **Validation Rules** tab.
5. Click the **New Validation Rule** button. The **Create Validation Rule** popup appears.
6. Choose the field for which you want the rule to apply.
7. For example, you might want a Validation Rule to ensure the state field only have 2 characters or that a discount be between 15 and 25 percent.
8. Click Next. The **Validation Rule Editor** opens.
9. Select an **Execute** rule from the drop-down list and specify the criteria for validation.
10. For the example above you would select **Number of Characters** for the **Execute Rule** and 2 for the **criterion**.
11. Click **Done**.
12. Enter the **alert message** to display when records meet the condition.
13. For example, you could add a message like, "Try that again, buddy. We don't allow discounts over 25%" to help build morale.
14. Click **Save** to save the validation rule.

Fig 6-3 Creating a Validation Rule

Workflow Rules

Workflow Rules are a set of actions that execute when certain conditions are met. These rules automate processes like sending email notifications, assigning tasks and updating certain fields when a rule is triggered.

There are numerous times when you may want to use a Workflow Rule. You might look around your office and focus on your repetitive tasks. Do you have a process for working with new leads? Do you have an onboarding process for new customers? Do you want to have something special happen when a deal closes? These are all times when you might consider creating a Workflow Rule.

A workflow rule consists of three parts:

- **When:** When do you want this action to happen?
- **Condition:** What triggers the action?
- **Action:** What do you want to happen?

A great way to better understand Workflow is to take a look at the one that Zoho CRM provides you with: The ***Big Deal Rule***. This rule is set to trigger when a Deal is created or edited to include an amount of over $1,000 and a probability of 100%. When these conditions are met, a templated email goes out to any Users with the CEO role.

To create a new Workflow Rule:

1. Click the **Setup Gear**. The **Setup** page opens.
2. Click **Workflow Rules** in the Automation area. You will be on the Workflow Rules page.
3. Click **Create Rule**. The **Create New Rule** popup appears.
4. Select the **Module** to which the rule applies from the drop-down list, the **Rule Name** and an optional **Description**.
5. Click **Next**.

6. Select **"When"** and click **Next** to continue.

    Workflow Rules can be created for any Zoho CRM module, and can be set to activate based on one of the following criteria:

    - ✓ **On a Record Action** such as creating, editing, deleting a record, or updating a field.
    - ✓ **On a Date or Time** based on any of your time fields and can reoccur either monthly or yearly.
    - ✓ **Based On Score** that is either increased, decreased or updated.

7. Set your **Conditions** and click **Next**.

    You have a choice of running the rule for All Records or just the records that match your specific conditions after you create the Rule. You can create multiple conditions for a Workflow Rule. Each condition consists of both a query of your records and an action.

8. Create an **Action**.

    You can choose from a variety of Actions including updating a field, sending an email or creating a Task. You can also decide if you want the action to occur right away or at a scheduled time.

9. Click **Save** to save your Workflow Rule.

Not sure if your Workflow Rules are running as designed? Take a trip to the Audit Log to do your due diligence.

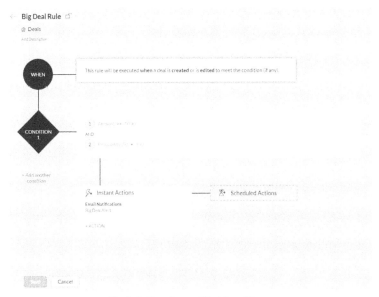

Fig 6-4 Creating a Workflow Room

Singing the Blueprint Blues

From the moment you capture a Lead, your organization has several processes in place. Each of these processes more than likely has several stages, and different teams may be responsible to complete each stage along the way.

Many CRM implementations fail because the processes in your software do not match the processes set by your company. Enter Blueprint. Zoho CRM's Blueprint helps you create a flowchart of your business processes, like what you would create in software such as Visio, Mind Map or even Excel.

Creating a Blueprint is a three-step process:

- ➢ Enter the basic information.
- ➢ Define the process.
- ➢ Configure the transitions.

Here's how to start your Blueprint:

1. Click the **Setup Gear**. The **Setup** page opens.
2. Click **Blueprint** in the **Process Management** area. The **Blueprint** window will open. You'll see that there are already two Blueprints that you can play with to get a feel for this feature.

3. Click the **Create Blueprint** icon. The **Create new Blueprint** popup window opens.

4. Name the **Blueprint**.

5. Choose the Module, Layout and field for which the process is being created.

   As an example, if you want to create a Blueprint for Quotes, choose the Quotes Module, and select the Quote Stage field.

6. (Optional) Define your **criteria**.

   For example, your criteria might include Quotes that are in a certain stage. If you don't enter criteria, all records created in the layout enter the process.

7. Click **Next**. The **Drag & Drop States** page opens.

   Here's where the fun begins. The object of the game is to drag the various *states* on to the work surface and then connect them with *transitions*. A state is the various choices for the field you selected in Step 5 above. A transition denotes actions that need to occur before, during and after an event.

8. Drag and drop all the stages that form your process on to the canvas area of the **Drag & Drop States** page.

9. Hover your mouse along the bottom edge of a state and use the blue circle that appears to connect your states.

10. Create **Transitions** by clicking on the **Plus** icon between two States. You'll notice that when you click the **Plus** icon the **Transitions** tab opens on the right-hand side.

11. Name your Transition and click **Save**. The **Transition** tab will now include 3 sub-tabs:

    ✓ **Before:** This is where you specify the **Users** who are responsible to execute a Transition and define the **criteria** which determines exactly when this Transition should be available for the records in a process. If you have no such conditions, you can skip the criteria section; the Transition is visible on all records right away.

Batten Down the Hatches

- ✓ **During**: This is where you prompt your Users for an action. For example, you might prompt them to enter specific fields, notes, attachments and other information.

- ✓ **After:** This is where you determine the things that you want to happen automatically, such as updating a field value or sending an email notification.

12. (Optional) **Right-click** a **stage** or **transition** and choose **Delete** to remove an unwanted step.
13. Click **Publish** to start the Blueprint or **Save as Draft** to make further changes later.

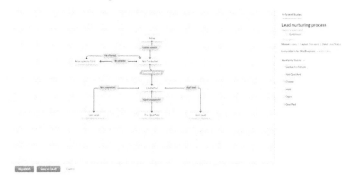

Fig 6-5 The Lead Nurturing Blueprint

Whew! There's an awful lot that goes into creating a Blueprint. Now that you understand the basic concepts, you might want to review the two existing Blueprints that came with Zoho CRM. This might give you a better understanding of how your new Blueprint can be improved.

Data Administration for the Database Administrator

This chapter is devoted to the Zoho CRM database administrator who, in addition to having to periodically remind users how to retrieve a forgotten password, is also responsible for ensuring the data remains safe and sound. Zoho CRM gives you several tools to make that job much easier.

Database Backup

If you did any research on Zoho prior to your purchase, then you know your data is extremely safe. However, it's better to be safe than sorry. Most Zoho editions come with at least two backups per month. You have the option to purchase additional backups if needed. Best of all, you can automate the backup process. The data backup creation can take as little as a few minutes to as much as several hours, depending on the database size.

You might be surprised to see the amount of data contained in your backup. In the rare case that you migrate from Zoho CRM to another CRM product, everything you need is in one simple spot. If you've ever worked with other CRM product backups or migrations, you might be surprised at how easy and comprehensive the Zoho CRM backup is, especially considering that there was no cost involved.

Follow these steps to schedule a data backup:

1. Click the **Setup Gear**. The **Setup** page opens.
2. Click **Data Backup** in the Data Administration area.
3. Click the **Backup Preference** button.
4. Click the **radio button** to choose when the backup should take place and then click **Done**. The **Backup Summary** appears, showing the type of backup chosen, status of backup and when the next backup is scheduled.

Zoho notifies you when the backup is finished. Your download link is active for 7 days. Once the data backup is ready, the User with administrative privileges can download it.

To download your backup:

1. Click the **Setup Gear**. The **Setup** page opens.
2. Click **Data Backup** in the Data Administration area.
3. Click the file listed in the **Download** section to download it.

The data and the attachments are compressed into separate .zip folders: one with your actual data and one with your attachments.

I Think We Need an Audit

The Audit Log is a list of the events performed by Users in Zoho CRM. Only users assigned an Administrator level profile can access the Audit Log.

The Audit Log tracks actions performed for the last 60 days including:

- ➤ Records that have been added, updated or deleted.
- ➤ Imported and exported records.
- ➤ Lead conversions.
- ➤ Deduped records.

To access the Audit Log:

1. Click the **Setup Gear**. The **Setup** page opens.

2. Click **Audit Log** in the **Data Administration** area. The Audit Log page opens.

3. (Optional) Click the **Filter by** icon next to **Recent Activity**.

   Since the Audit Log is quite exhaustive, it can be challenging to sift through all the entries if you are looking for a few specific details. For example, you may only want to see the records added by a particular User or a list of all changes performed in the last 2 days.

4. Select your filtering options:

   Entity: Select the Module that you want to view.

   User: Provide the name of the User that you want to spy on.

   Action: Here's where you can view the added, edited or deleted records.

   Time: Give a time frame.

5. (Optional) Click the **Export Audit Log** to create and download a CSV copy of the Audit Log.

It is easy to delete records in Zoho CRM. Fortunately, it's just as easy to recover them! The ***Recycle Bin*** stores all the records from all the CRM modules as well as any attachments that are deleted from the **Zoho** CRM. The records in the **recycle bin** will be available for 60 days after which it will be permanently deleted from your help desk account.

1. Click the Setup **Gear** in the Tab bar.

2. Click **Recycle Bin** under the **Data** Administration area of the Setup page.

3. Select the check boxes of the records that you want to restore In the **Recycle Bin**.

You'll notice that Zoho CRM provides you with the type of item that was deleted as well as the person who deleted the item along with the deletion date and time. Talk about being caught red-handed!

4. Click **Restore**.

   If there seems to be a lot of information that you are having to fish out of the Recycle Bin you might consider taking a look at the Security Profiles you have setup and remove the ability to delete data.

Fig 6-6 Restoring the Recycle Bin

Now if there were only an easy way to take back some of the things we've inadvertently said!

Houston, We Have a Problem!

According to Zoho's **Service Level Agreement** (SLA), Zoho guarantees a monthly uptime of 99.9%. This excludes any downtime caused by scheduled maintenance and updates "which will be communicated well in advance". However, if you expect that Zoho will never experience a downtime, your expectations are a bit unrealistic. You can be assured that should an outage happen Zoho's track record shows that it will be fixed very quickly.

If your users are complaining of an outage you can check the status of all the Zoho products at **status.zoho.com**. You will see a listing of all products that are experiencing issues; drill down on an outage and you will see the exact locations that are infected.

Worried about outages? You can subscribe to the status page and receive updates by email or text.

Let's Head to the Marketplace

The Marketplace is a place where you can download products to extend the power of Zoho CRM. Some of these products are free and some include a price tag. The Marketplace is divided into four areas:

- All
- Zoho
- Google
- Microsoft

The **Google** and **Microsoft** areas are pretty much what you would expect. They house add-in tools for Google and Microsoft products. **All** houses just about everything you could think of.

The one area that you need to be aware of is the Zoho area. Unlike the other areas of the Marketplace, this is where you find integrations to other Zoho products. For example, this is where you find integration to sync your Contacts and Accounts to Zoho Books.

To get to the Marketplace:

1. Click the **Setup Gear** in the Tab bar.
2. Click the desired area under the **Marketplace** area of the **Setup** page.

7

Sending Email Blasts

On the simplest level you can use Zoho CRM as a glorified rolodex and be quite happy with a place to find basic contact information. However, if you're at all interested in growing, or maintaining the size of, your business you'll want to make use of mass mailing.

The number of mass emails that you can send will vary based on your Zoho CRM Edition:

- Standard Edition: 250/day.
- Professional Edition: 500/day.
- Enterprise Edition: 1,000/day.

If you have Zoho One, your CRM is the Enterprise Edition. You can send 1,000 emails/day to your closest friends and acquaintances. Remember that this limit includes autoresponders and other scheduled emails you have setup.

If you need to send more than your daily limit, you can segment your recipients into smaller groups and mail to one group per day. You can also increase this limit for a nominal fee. Alternatively, you can use Zoho Campaigns, Zoho's email marketing application and go above the daily limit.

Sending an email blast involves a few steps:

- Decide to whom your sending
- Create a template
- Send the email blast
- Review the emailing analytics

Creating CRM Email Templates

Before you can win friends and influence prospects with your dazzling display of personalized e-mail documents you need two things: data and a document template.

The data part is easy. By now you have added records to the Lead and Contact modules. Hopefully you've added a few key fields so that you can now easily *segment* your database. But you might be confused by the word *template*.

Quite simply, a template is a time saver. Templates save you retyping an email you might use often. It might even contain merge fields that are then filled in with information from your database. Using Zoho CRM to create e-mail templates enables you to quickly blast out frequently sent emails, and to send a personalized e-mail to each recipient.

Using the Template Gallery

If you've never created a template, you might start with one of the pre-existing templates. Zoho CRM comes with dozens of example templates. This makes your life a whole lot easier and each template is completely customizable. All you have to do is drag and drop components on the template to modify it. The predefined templates even include some basic, "graphic-less" templates, suitable for text-only, everyday needs. You can even import HTML or create a Plain Text email.

To access the Template Gallery:

1. Click the **Setup Gear**. The **Setup** page opens.

2. Click **Templates** in the **Customization** area. You will be on the **Email** tab of the **Templates** page.

3. Click the **+ New Template** button. The **Create Email Template** popup window appears.

4. Select the desired Module from the **Select Module** dropdown and then click **Next**. The **Template Gallery** opens.

    In Zoho CRM, email templates are module specific; they are created for a specific record type. For example, you can create a template specific to your Leads and another one to be used with your Contacts. When you send emails to lead records, only the templates created for lead records will be available for merging.

5. Scroll through the templates, or click a category from the **Vertical Navigation Bar,** until you find the one that best suits your needs.

   The Templates are divided into the following categories:

   - ✓ Basic
   - ✓ Celebration
   - ✓ Invitation
   - ✓ Followup
   - ✓ Product Promotion
   - ✓ Notification

   Remember, the goal of this drill is to find a template that is closest to what you are looking for. All the templates are customizable. You can remove unwanted elements, and replace the graphics with your own. If you are looking for a newsletter template, consider choosing one of the **Basic** templates. Choose the **Blank** template if you want to start entirely from scratch.

6. (Optional) Change the Module in the **Template Gallery Horizontal Navigation Bar.**

   You can create templates for any of the Zoho CRM modules including Quotes, Cases, and even phone calls.

7. (Optional) To preview a template, click the **Magnifying Glass** that appears when you hover your mouse over a template.

8. To select a template, click the **Select** button that appears when you hover your mouse over a template.

9. Enter a **Template Name** and a **Template Subject** in the top left corner of the **Horizontal Navigation Bar.** The maximum length for a template name is 75 characters; the maximum length for a subject is 150 characters.

10. Click the **Save** button.

11. Select the appropriate folder from the **Save To** dropdown, or chose **New Folder** to create a new folder for your template.

    By now you might be growing weary of the repeated

warnings to keep your data organized. This is particularly important when it comes to creating templates. By creating template folders, you can organize your templates and find them again easily. Consider creating a folder for your news letters and another one for marketing pieces.

Enter the name of the new folder and choose with whom the folder will be shared. You can choose to share it with all users, specific users, or just yourself. A new folder will be created, and the template will get added to it automatically.

12. Click **Save** to save your template.

Fig 7-1 The Leads Template Gallery

Tweaking Existing Templates

Using Zoho CRM's template library is a great way to save time. However, chances are slim that one of the existing templates is exactly what you were looking for. Not to worry; it's very easy to change existing templates.

1. Click the **Setup Gear**. The **Setup** page opens.

2. Click **Templates** in the **Customization** area. You will be on the **Email** tab of the **Templates** page.

3. Click the **Pencil** icon to the right of the template would like to edit.

4. Click a desired component from the **All Components** section; the **All Components** section will slide away to present you with more options.

    For example, if you want to select Button, you will see three size options. If you select Background, you will be asked to change the outer or inner background

5. (Optional) **Drag** any additional components onto the template and customize it as needed.

6. Click on a **Text Box** to change the wording of the template.

   As you click a Text Box, you'll notice the **formatting tool bar** appear at the top of the screen. You'll probably recognize the icons for font and alignment changes. If you're not sure of any of them, just hover your mouse over an icon to see a tooltip.

   You might also notice the Create Link icon; here's where you can add the following hyperlink types to your template:

   - ✓ Web URL
   - ✓ Email
   - ✓ Unsubscribe Link

7. (Optional) **Add merge fields** to personalize your template by typing a **#** to open a list of merge fields for the selected module.

   You can greatly Increase the deliverability of your blast by personalizing it. An email that starts with a personalized greeting such as "Dear John" has a much better chance of making it through spam filters than a message without personalization.

8. (Optional) Click the **Attachments** link to add an attachment to your template. You can attach a maximum of 10 files with a total size limit of 3MB.

9. Click **Save** to save your template.

   If you are editing a previously saved template, the **Add Comments** popup window will open prompting you to add a comment. Whenever changes are made to a template, it is considered as a new version. Zoho CRM keeps track of every version change; these comments will appear in the Audit Log. You can also look at separate analytics for each version of your template.

Zoho CRM Essentials

Fig 7-2 Happy Holidays Template

Cloning a Template to Another Module

You might find yourself wanting to send a similar template to different Zoho CRM modules. For example, you might create a newsletter template and wish to send it to both Contact and Lead records. If that's the case, cloning a template is the perfect solution.

To clone a template:

1. Click the **Setup Gear**. The **Setup** page opens.

2. Click **Templates** in the **Customization** area. You will be on the **Email** tab of the **Templates** page.

3. Click the **name** of the template that you wish to clone. A preview of the template will open.

4. Click the **Clone** icon to the right of the template preview. The **Clone Template** page window will open.

5. (Optional) Give the new template a new Template Name. If you do not provide a new name, then the previous one will be used, with _**Cloned** affixed to the template's name.

6. (Optional) Create a new subject line for the template.

7. (Optional) Create new merge fields that correspond to the new module.

    Any merge fields you had included in the original template will now appear highlighted in red along with a banner warning across the top of the template to remove them. You will have to delete and add new merge fields that reflect the fields in the new module.

8. Click **Save**. The **Save Template** popup window opens.
9. (Optional) Change the **Template Name** and the **Save To** folder.
10. Click **Save** to save the newly cloned template.

Sending Templated Email

Once you've finished with the heavy lifting of creating a template, sending it is a relatively easy task.

Templates can be used in two ways:

> - **To a single record:** For example, you might routinely send thank-you e-mails to your Contacts. You would also like them to be personalized with their first name, and send them out on an "as-needed" basis.
>
> - **As a Mass Email:** An example of this would be sending out an announcement or a promotion about one of your products.

Once sent, you can see basic analytics, including the Open Rate and the Click Rate, based on Template Version. This is great for testing the efficiency of similar, but slightly different, emails.

Sending a Template One Record at a Time

Many Zoho CRM users associate a template with an email blast and overlook the amount of time a template can save. Think of emails you send on a routine basis: introductions, common responses to questions about your products and services, and follow-ups. Rather than re-inventing the wheel each time, you should use a template.

To send an email to a single contact:

1. **Search** for the record to whom you would like to send an email template.
2. Click the **Send Email** button. The **New Message** popup window appears.

   You'll notice that your daily send limit appear at the bottom of the window.

3. Click the Insert link and select **Template**.

4. Click the **name** of the template you wish to send.

   The template appears; any merge fields in the template are populated with the corresponding data from the contact's record.
   Not seeing your template? Remember, templates are specific to modules. If you created a template for Leads, it will not appear if you are attempting to mail to a Contact record.

5. Click **Send**.

The email template opens for your perusal. Need to tweak it? Tweak away by adding a comment or changing some of the wording.

Sending Templated Emails to Multiple Records

It is easy to send your template to multiple records selected from an existing list view. In this example, you want to send the same email message to multiple recipients. If you've already created Custom Views, this is an easy starting point to hand-selecting recipients:

1. Select any **Module**.

2. Specify a **Custom View** or **Filter**.

3. Select all records by clicking the **Checkbox** at the top of the List View, to the left of your column headings.

You may have to click the **Select All records in this view** link. In the top right of your List View, the number of Records selected is displayed.

4. Click the **Send Email** button. The **Mass Email** popup window opens.

   Don't see this option? You probably selected more than your allotted number of records. Just to make sure you are on the right track, the Mass Email window displays the number of emails (if any) sent today.

5. Click **Select Template**. The **Select Template** popup window opens.

Sending Email Blasts

6. Select the name of your template. The **Mass Email** popup window opens.

7. (Optional) Change the **Reply To** email if you want to send replies to a different user.

8. Select one of the **Send Options**. You have two choices:

    ✓ Send Immediately: Zoho CRM will instantly send out the email.

    ✓ **Schedule Later:** Select the date and time that you would like Zoho CRM to use to send out the email.

9. (Optional) Click the **Trigger an action** link to Setup Follow-up Actions.

    The Triggers include:

    ✓ Email is opened

    ✓ Email is clicked

    ✓ Email is bounced

    If you choose one of the first two triggers, you can tell Zoho CRM to Update Fields, add a Follow-up Task, or Schedule a Call. If you choose the third, Email is bounced option, you can have Zoho CRM update one or more of your fields.

9. Click **Send** if your send option is to **Send Immediately**; click **Schedule** if your send option is set to **Schedule Later**.

Fig 7-3 Sending a Mass Email

Sending with All the Bells and Whistles

By now you realize that there are numerous ways to use your templates. However, there is one more trick up the Zoho CRM sleeve: fully automated, targeted Mass Emails. This is a perfect combination of powerful and easy!

An email marketing rule of thumb is that the more targeted your list, the greater the results. Consider an engine repair guy who can service anything from cars to airplanes. If that repair guy sends an email about airplane repairs to a car owner, it will probably lead to a lot of confusion, and very little engagement.

The major differences between sending an email template to a list, filter, or hand-selected records, like we did in the previous section, and the full-fledge Mass Email feature, are:

- **Recipients**: You can target Custom List Views or create a specific criterion "on the fly."
- **Follow-up Actions:** You can create any number of follow-up emails or activities.

Here's how to use Mass Email:

1. On the **Horizontal Navigation** Bar click the name of the module to which you want to send a mass email. This will open the module's **Home** page.
2. Click the **Actions** button and select **Mass Email.** The Mass Email page opens.
3. Click the **Create Mass Email** link. The **New Mass Email** page opens.
4. Specify the **details** for the **Mass Email**.
5. These details are identical to the steps you follow when sending an email template to multiple records.
6. Select an option from the **To** option.
7. Select one of your **Custom List Views** or click **Based on Criteria** to create a query on the fly.
8. (Optional) Click **Add Follow-up** to schedule additional emails. The Follow-up popup window opens.
9. This is what separates the men from the boys – or the **Send Email** option from the **Mass Email** option. You have

Sending Email Blasts

four questions to answer:

- ✓ **Who should receive this email?** You have a choice of selecting the folks who received the email, or the folks that actually opened it.
- ✓ **Do you want to ignore any contacts from receiving this follow-up email?** This step is totally optional.
- ✓ **Which email template should be used?** You can either choose an existing template or create a new one.
- ✓ **When should the follow-up email be sent?** You can schedule the next email on either a specific day, or a specific number of days, after the initial send.

9. Once done, click **Add**. The follow-up email will appear in the **Follow-up Emails** section. You can create as many follow-up emails as needed.

10. Click **Send** or **Schedule** to send the Mass Email.

Fig 7-4 Sending a Mail Merge

Sending a template is half the fun; the second half comes from measuring the success of your send. Zoho CRM's template analytics shows the performance of each template, and each version of a template. This lets you analyze how well each version of the template performed. As an example, you might spend a great deal of time developing "eye-catching" templates loaded with graphics, only to discover that your plain vanilla, text-only templates, garner a much higher open rate.

111

Luckily for you, by following these steps, Zoho CRM makes it very easy to see how well your template did.

1. Click the **Setup Gear**. The **Setup** page opens.

2. Click **Templates** in the **Customization** area. You will be on the **Email** tab of the **Templates** page.

3. Click **percentage,** under the **STATS** column, for the template you want to analyze. The **Open Rate Tab** opens, showing a graph with the template statistics.

   The Open Rate is the percentage of recipients who *open* a specific email template, out of your total number sent. If the open rate is low, it probably means your subject line needs improvement, or that the recipients are viewing your incoming message as a sales pitch.

4. (Optional) Click the **mini-calendars** on the top of the graph to define the range of dates for the graph.

5. (Optional) Scroll through the dates using the **Next** and **Previous** arrows to the right of the graph.

6. Click the **Click Rate Tab**.

   The Click Rate is the percentage of emails where a link or button was clicked. If the click rate is low, it may mean that your recipients weren't compelled by your messaging.

7. Click the **Version Tab**.

   The Version tab gives you a list, by date of the template versions along with the comments, and the name of the user that made the changes. Each version will have its own open rate and click rate.

Sending Email Blasts

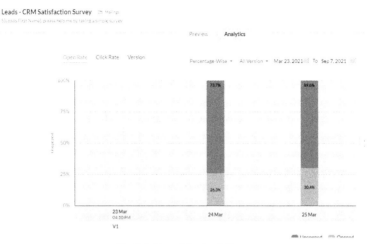

Fig 7-5 Template Analytics

Campaigning Doesn't Just Occur in an Election Year

For most of you, the Email and Mass Email functionality included in Zoho CRM mailing may be more than enough. However, if you want a full-fledged marketing product, with full opt-out and bounce management, detailed statistics, and fully conditional email marketing automation, or if you just need a much higher send allotment, **Zoho Campaigns** is the best way to go.

Zoho Campaigns is a separate Zoho application that includes everything you can do in with Zoho CRM email features, and then some:

- ➢ **Templates:** Zoho CRM has a number of templates; Zoho Campaigns has far more, with new ones added all the time. Unfortunately, Zoho CRM templates are not accessible in Zoho Campaigns.
- ➢ **Send Limit:** The send limit increases from 1,000 emails/day in CRM's Enterprise Edition, to a whooping 100,000 sends per month in Zoho Campaigns, depending on your Campaigns version.
- ➢ **Subscriber Management:** Yes, Virginia, you can access all your CRM records in Zoho Campaigns. And you can see Campaigns results in the Related List for any CRM module. With Zoho Campaigns, you can also import lists from other sources and email to those as well.

- **Signup Forms:** Create templated sign-up forms for your website, or collect emails from a website popup form.
- **Ecommerce:** You can connect your Zoho Commerce, Shopify, BigCommerce, or WooCommerce store. This will allow you to automate your processes by sending promotional emails about your products, abandoned-cart emails, and purchase follow-ups.
- **Reporting and Analytics:** You can use one of the many reports that come with Zoho Campaigns, or you can connect Zoho Campaigns to Zoho Analytics, to access even more reports and dashboards.

You can add Zoho Campaigns to your subscription at **TechBenders.com/Campaigns**, or if you are a Zoho One subscriber, it is included free of charge.

Let's Make a Deal

In this chapter, I lead you through the entire Zoho CRM sales process. I show you how to create an initial Deal, edit it the Deal as it makes its way through the sales pipeline, and view your opportunities via the Deal List. In addition, you can view the Deal from any Contact, Account, or related record. As if that weren't enough, there are a slew of Analytics dashboards and Reports, ranging from the basic Today's Sales to the Salesperson's Performance Report. Whew!

In Zoho CRM, a **Deal** is a potential sale or opportunity. All sales information for a Deal appears in the Deals Detail page. When you create a Deal, you can specify a sales stage and forecasted close date, and make use of customizable fields. You can even schedule a follow-up activity or create a note for the deal.

By tracking the sales process using Zoho CRM, you have a better chance of closing more sales. First, if you follow up on your activities, you have significantly fewer contacts falling through the cracks. Secondly, you can adjust your predictions while the deal moves through the various sales stages. Most importantly, you can filter the Deal List, allowing you to focus on the deals that you think you have the best chance of closing.

You can associate a Deal with additional record types, typically Contact and Account records. You can associate a Deal with only one account, but you can associate it with multiple contacts. For example, you might be working with one person who is the Decision Maker, another that will get you paid, and another who is the person that will implement a project.

Zoho CRM's Deals module is very customizable; this should be done prior to adding any deals to your database. You can add new fields to the Deals Module as well as change the layout – or create new ones – using the exact same method you use when create new Account, Contact, or Lead fields. You can also add an additional pipeline if you need one, and change the existing Deal Stages.

Creating Multiple Pipelines

A sales *pipeline* is a visual display of your Deals. It shows where your prospects are in the buying cycle, how many open deals you have, how long a particular deal stayed in each stage, and whether you have a good chance of winning or losing a deal. A pipeline is set to a specific set of stages. Your company might have multiple pipelines. For example, you might work with governmental entities which usually have a long and slow sales process, and with small businesses which typically have faster and simpler transactions.

Working with multiple pipelines can get a bit confusing. A pipeline is associated with a specific layout. As an example, you might have one pipeline associated with your sales layout, and another pipeline associated with your marketing layout. However, you can also create multiple pipelines for a single layout:

1. Click the **Setup Gear**. The Setup page opens.
2. Click **Pipelines** in the **Customization** area. The Manage Pipelines page opens.
3. Select the layout that will contain the new pipeline.
4. (Optional) Rename the existing pipeline by clicking on the name changing it from Standard which is the default Pipeline name.
5. Click **Create New Pipeline**. The Create Pipeline popup window will popup.
6. Give a Name to your new pipeline to identify it from your other pipeline(s).
7. Select the **Stages** for the new pipeline by clicking on any of the existing stages.
8. You'll see a list of all your existing stages, or you can create a new one by clicking **Create New Stage**.
9. (Optional) click the **Set as Default** checkbox if you would like to make this your default pipeline.
10. Click **Save** to save your new pipeline.

Let's Make a Deal

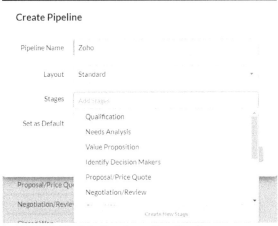

Fig 8-1 Creating a New Pipeline

Once you create a new pipeline, make sure that you use it properly. Here are a few things to keep in mind:

> ➢ Select the appropriate pipeline when creating a new deal. Alternatively, if you have recently created a new pipeline, you can globally move existing deals to the new pipeline based on your selection criteria.
>
> ➢ The Deal List View can be filtered by pipeline. To make it easy to access your pipelines, you might consider creating and saving a Filter or View..
>
> ➢ For additional clarity you might want to add the pipeline column to the Deal List View.

Customizing the Deal Stages

Zoho Deal stages allow you to set up the steps your organization follows when trying to close a sale. You can even associate a probability with each Stage. It's rumored that you need to contact someone 12 times before you convert them from a prospect to a customer; here's where you can be reminded of where you are in that process.

The out of the box Deal Stages are fairly generic and apply to most businesses. However, your business might do things its own, unique way. If that's the case, customize the existing Deal Stages and make them your own:

1. Click the **Setup Gear**. The **Setup** page opens.

2. Click **Modules and Fields** in the **Customization** area. You will be on the **Modules Tab**.

3. **Hover** your mouse to the right of the **Deal Module** and select **Stage-Probability Mapping**. The **Stage-Probability** window will open.

The Stage-Probability Mapping window is divided into three columns: Stage Name, Probability, Forecast Type and Forecast Category. At first glance the Stage-Probability Mapping window is a bit cluttered because there is a lot of information jammed into each row. Just take your time until you feel comfortable making changes.

4. Make the basic changes.

   - ✓ **Rename a Stage:** Click on a Stage Name and change it.
   - ✓ **Add a Stage:** Click the **Plus** icon to the right of a **Stage Name** to add a new stage below the existing one.
   - ✓ **Delete a Stage:** Click the **Minus** icon to the right of a Stage Name to remove a stage.
   - ✓ **Reorder the Stages: Drag** the field handle to the right of a **Stage Name** to the desired location.
   - ✓ **Choose a Pipeline**: Decide how you would like the stage categorized when you are running pipeline reports. You may choose to Omit a stage, or consider certain stages to indicate that a Deal is Closed.

5. Provide a **Probability** percentage.

Zoho has a weighted sales pipeline feature. As a Deal progresses through the pipeline, it has higher chance of closing. As an example, new deals might have a 10% chance of closing, whereas deals that have already negotiated pricing might have an 80% chance of closing. The ***probability*** is multiplied by the ***deal amount*** to give you the ***expected revenue***.

6. Select a **Forecast Type**. Forecasts types are categories used to segment deals in CRM's Sales Forecasting, and for segmenting Deals in reports and Analytics.

7. Click **Save** to save your changes.

Creating a Deal

Here is a quick-tour of the Deal details page:

1. Click **Deals** in the Horizontal Navigation Bar.

2. In the **Deals** module, click **New Deal**. Alternatively, you can hover over **Deals** from a Contact's **Related Lists** area and **click** the **Plus** icon.

3. In the **Create Deal** page, enter the important deal details. Only a few of them are required; they are easy to spot as they have a red border.

    - ✓ **Deal Name:** Try to come up with something easy to recall the deal. Using the Account Name or Contact Name is a bit superfluous as you can also associate a deal with a specific account or contact.

    - ✓ **Account Name:** By default, Deals are required to be associated with a specific account. If you sell direct to consumer, this can be disabled.

    - ✓ **Closing Date:** Indicate your best guesstimate of when the deal will close. Remember, you can always update this as needed.

    - ✓ **Stage:** If you don't assign a specific stage, Zoho CRM automatically assigns the deal to the first stage in your pipeline.

4. Add the **Amount**.

    Give your best estimate as to the value of the deal. The whole purpose of a pipeline is to help you to pinpoint the best sources of expected revenue. This amount can easily be changed as you go through the negotiation process.

    The **Expected Revenue** field is automatically calculated and cannot be manually edited. This field represents the value of the **Amount** multiplied by the **Probability** percentage.

5. (Optional) Select the correct pipeline from the Pipeline field drop-down if your company has multiple pipelines.

6. Click **Save** to save your new deal.

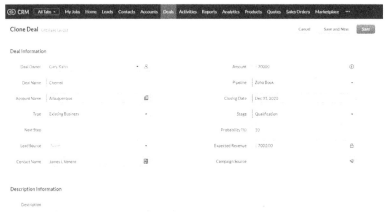

Fig 8-2 Creating a Deal

Imagine Zoho CRM as a series of building blocks. Once you've mastered one aspect you've actually mastered a dozen others as well. This holds particularly true with Deals. You can view a deal's history by looking at the Timeline in the Deals Detail page. You can also create deal-specific activities and notes to make ensure that your deal moves quickly through the pipeline.

Modifying the Deal

Deals by nature should move through stages or milestones. Updating the stage becomes a necessary step. Again, this information appears in your various reports, so updating your opportunities is vitally important. This process is quick and painless.

1. **Search** for the **Deal** that you wish to modify.

   There are actually a few ways to do this. You might search for an Account or Contact record, and then access the Deal from the Related List area. You can also search for a Deal by its name, if you know it.

2. **Click** the appropriate **Stage** from the progress bar across the top of the **Deal Details** page.

3. Click in any field to **Edit** the Deal details. Click the blue check button to save the field edit.

4. (Optional) If you need to change multiple fields, click the **Edit** button in the upper right to open all fields for editing. Remember, you will not be able to modify the Expected Revenue field as it is based on a calculation. Click **Save** to save your changes.

In Zoho CRM there are very often several ways to accomplish a task. If you prefer a more visual approach, you might try viewing your Deals in the Kanban view. Using the Kanban, you can simply "slide" your deals from one stage to another by clicking and dragging.

Set up Big Deal Alert

You can use the ***Big Deal Alert*** to notify other users about your successes. These Big-deal alerts can take the form of an e-mail notification to some or all of your Zoho CRM users, or even to folks that are not registered Zoho CRM users. By default, there is a Big Deal Alert in Zoho CRM that you can modify and use. Unfortunately, these alerts don't come equipped with pay raises and additional time-off.

To configure big deal alert:

1. Click the **Setup Gear**. The **Setup** opens.

2. Click **Workflow Rules** in the **Automation** area. You will be on the **Workflow Rules** page.

3. Click **Big Deal Rule** from the list of rules. The **Big Deal Rule** page opens. This is a great way to become acquainted with the concept of workflow rules. You'll notice that the rule contains three sections.

    - ✓ **When:** This defines when you want the action to occur.
    - ✓ **Condition(s):** This clarifies the conditions that must be met
    - ✓ **Action(s):** This defines what you want to happen.

4. Click the **Pencil** in the upper right corner of each text box and make your changes. For example, you might want an email to go out when a new deal is created that is over $10,000. Or you might want to have a field updated when a new deal is created.

5. Click **Save** to save your changes. You will be back on the Workflow Rules page.

6. Make sure the workflow **Status** is set to **Green** as in "show me the money!"

Once you get the hang of editing the Big Deal Rule, creating additional rules becomes even easier. You can clone an existing rule, make a few changes, and voila – you are the brand-new owner of another workflow rule!

9

Show Me the Money

So far, you've learned how to setup a database, do a bit of marketing, and even get a feel for when something good is about to happen. This chapter explores what to do to get money flowing through your doors. Specifically, you'll learn how to add Products to Zoho CRM, and create a Quote using those Products. If that isn't enough to get your juices flowing, you can send out that Quote, receive a payment, and log the receipt in Zoho Books to see the money in your bank account.

You might be confused between the invoicing tools that are in Zoho CRM and those that are in the Zoho Finance Suite. You are not alone; it *is* a bit confusing! Zoho CRM includes the modules that you need to send quotes and receive payments including:

➢ Products

➢ Quotes

➢ Invoices

➢ Purchase Orders

➢ Sales Orders

However, you might find these tools to be a bit basic for your purposes. Although these modules can send invoices and collect payments, the payments are not tied into your accounting system, leaving you with an incomplete picture of your finances.

You might be using another accounting solution such as QuickBooks. If that's the case you might already be used to logging invoices and payments. However, if you want the whole enchilada – a world where your CRM talks to your accounting system - you'll want to consider the **Zoho Finance Suite** which is included as part of Zoho One.

- ➢ Zoho Books
- ➢ Zoho Expense
- ➢ Zoho Subscriptions
- ➢ Zoho Inventory

Zoho Books is the core piece of the Finance Suite. It is basically a fully functional accounting program that includes everything you need, down to the last debit and credit. If a company uses Zoho Books they can pretty much kiss double-entry accounting goodbye. The components of the Zoho Finance Suite are also more advanced. For example, if you need a comprehensive inventory for your company, the Inventory component included in the Finance Suite has more features than the one built into Zoho CRM. The Finance Suite is included with your Zoho One subscription.

As enticing as the Finance Suite sounds, many companies are unwilling or unable to take the plunge and bid farewell to their current accounting system. If that's the case, you'll use the Zoho CRM tools. You can update to the more complete versions at any time. And rest assured, all your Zoho CRM information will upgrade seamlessly from Zoho CRM to Zoho Finance Suite. You can sign up for Zoho Books at **TechBenders.com/Books**

Adding Products Will Make You More Productive

The Products module helps you to create and manage products for your company. When you create a Quote, you can either select one of the products from your product list, or can just fill in product information "on the fly." Although the idea of filling in product information as you go might seem appealing at first glance, it is well worth the effort to create a product list prior to creating your first Quote or Invoice. Creating products in advance ensures that Quote or Invoice line items are accounted for properly. The Product List also helps you designate which products are subject to sales tax. Products in the Product List can also be neatly arranged into custom categories.

We will concentrate on the Products module that is embedded in Zoho CRM. However, as you get more enmeshed into Zoho CRM, you might find that your products require a little more pizazz. Perhaps you want to bundle several products into a specially discounted "package." Maybe some of your products have special attributes such as a size or a color that you need to monitor. You might even want to create a price list to make it easy to see the prices you give to your best clients. All this can be done in the *Inventory* app which is part of *Zoho Books*. Needless to say, this is also where you'll want to head should you want to actually track your inventory.

Don't think that because your company doesn't sell widgets - or some similar item - that you can't use the Product List. Perhaps a better name for this field would've been Products/Services. At any rate, if you're gaining financially from your customers, use the Product List to help you analyze your profit centers.

To add a shiny new product:

1. Click **Products** from Zoho CRM's **Horizontal Navigation Bar**.

2. (Optional) If this is the first foray into the Products module, you will **click** the **Create a Product** button.

3. Click the **Plus** icon on the right side of the **Products Navigation Bar**.

4. **Enter** the product information on the **Create Product** page. The **Product Name** field is the only field that is required; the rest of the fields are optional. However, it's well worth your time to fill in as many fields as possible. A few of my favorites include:

    - ✓ **Product Code:** This can hold an SKU code or internal secret codes that are used to describe your product.

    - ✓ **Product Active:** Make sure this check box is selected if you want the newly created product to actually work. By default, the check box is selected.

    - ✓ **Unit Price:** Unless you possess an photographic memory, adding a unit price will help you to remember the correct cost of each of your products. It will also improve your math when you send out Quotes and Invoices; the quantity you input will automatically multiply with the unit price to give you a line-item total.

    - ✓ **Taxable:** The only certainties in life are death and

taxes - or so I'm told - and I'm fairly certain that if you sell products, you're going to have to pay taxes on them somewhere down the line. Zoho CRM takes the bitter edge off of taxes by providing you with a handy-dandy way of configuring which products are taxable with a single click.

- ✓ **Description:** Fill in a brief description of the Product; a bit of typing *now* will save you a ton of typing *later*!
- ✓ (Optional) Add a **Commission Rate.** This field will act as a calculator for any expression you input.
- ✓ (Optional) Add **Stock Information**. Here's where you can add things like the **Usage Unit** or **Quantity in Stock**. You can even indicate which of your users is going to make sure that you have a sufficient quantity in stock!

5. Click **Save** to save the Product.

You might already have a list of your products if you are using an accounting product such as QuickBooks. Keep in mind that you can import those products into Zoho CRM.

Fig 9-1 Creating a New Product

Clone Products if you Want to Save Time

You might find that many of your products are quite similar. Products can be "cloned." For example, you might sell widgets that come in red, white, or blue. The pricing is exactly the same for every widget; the only thing that changes is a slight tweak to the product's name and description. Here's how you can save yourself a lot of time:

1. Click the **Products** tab, and then select the product that you want to clone.
2. Click the **Ellipsis** and select **Clone**. The **Clone Product** page opens.
3. Modify the required details in the **Clone Product** page.
4. Click **Save** to save your changes.

You Can Quote Me on That

Wouldn't it be lovely if all your customers simply picked up the phone, placed an order, and ka-ching: the money was in the bank? Dream on! Many - if not all - of your customers are going to require, request, and/or demand that you send them a quote before they send you money. If that's the case with your business, you'll want to use the Quotes module that comes with Zoho CRM.

Quickly Creating Quotes

The Quotes module lets you create, view, and manage quotes for your organization. When you create a quote, you can select a product from the product catalog. Quotes specify the quantity and the price per unit for the products and services that you are selling to a customer. When you select a product, the system automatically fills in information such as the manufacturer's information and tax class.

Here's how you can go about creating quotes:

1. Open the record to which you would like to add a new Quote.

    You have a number of choices here; you can create a new quote from any of these locations:

    - ✓ From a Deal Record
    - ✓ From an Account Record
    - ✓ From a Contact Record

2. Click the **Plus** icon to the right of **Quotes** in the **Related Lists** area. The **Create Quote** page opens.

    You'll notice that if you start from an existing Deal, Account, or Contact record, most of the important details will already exist in the new quote.

3. Fill in any missing details.

   A few of the fields are required, including the Subject and Account Name fields. They will be easy to spot as required fields have a red line on the left boarder.

4. Click **Add Line Items** in the **Product Details** section. The **Choose Products** popup window opens.

5. Type in at least one character of the **Product Name,** or **Product Code,** in the **Choose Products** popup window, to see a list of your products.

6. (Optional) **Hover** your mouse over the **Info icon** next to the product to learn more about a product.

7. Enter the desired **Quantity** for the chosen product.

8. (Optional) Click the **Plus** icon to add more products to the quote. You can add up to 200 line items in a quote.

9. Click **Add Products** to add the products to the quote. All the details for the product, including taxes, discounts and product description, will populate automatically.

10. (Optional) To **reorder** line items, **drag** an item to the desired location by the handle on the item's right edge.

11. (Optional) **Hover** your mouse over a product to view the **unit price** and **quantity in stock**.

12. (Optional) Click the **Pencil** icon to the right of the **Discount** amount to add a discount to the relevant items.

    The **Set Discount** popup window opens. You can supply a discount based on a percentage or a dollar amount.

13. (Optional) Add **Terms and Conditions** and **Description Information** to the Quote.

14. Click **Save** to save your quote.

Fig 9-2 Creating a Quote

Sending a Quote

It's easy to create quotes in Zoho CRM. However, you'll probably also want to send them as well. You can email a quote by clicking the Email button at the top of the quote. An email will open with your Quote attached. The wording on the email is based on a template but you can easily change the wording prior to clicking Send. You can save the Quote as a .PDF file.

When you create a quote, it is automatically placed in *draft mode.* When a quote is in draft mode, it's an indication that it either needs to be approved or sent. Once the Quote is emailed to a contact, the status will change from Draft to Open.

Converting a Quote to a Sales Order or Invoice

To convert quotes to a sales order or invoice:

1. Click the **Quotes** tab on the **Horizontal Navigation Bar.**

2. Select the quote in the **Quotes Home** page. The **Quote Details** page opens.

3. Click **Convert**, and then select **Sales Order** or Invoice. The new **Sales Order** or **Invoice Details** page will appear.

If you have previously mapped fields between Quotes or Sales Orders and Invoices they automatically filled in on the new page. Invoices can be emailed in the same way you email a Quote, or can be saved as a PDF file.

I'm Between Projects Right Now

If your company is fairly small and your sales are transactional, you might not need any sort of project management. If that's the case, feel free to skip this chapter. However, if your sales are more complex and consist of many moving parts, you will probably want to add a bit of Project Management into the mix.

If you are a newbie, project management might consist of a pile of legal pads, sticky notes and folders strewn across your desk. If you have a Project Management Professional (PMP) certification you are already familiar with project management software. Whatever your situation, you can benefit from Zoho Projects, which contains most of the same functionality as competitive project management products, and is still simple enough for beginners.

Zoho Projects is designed to create and manage projects for your company. Working with Projects in Zoho Projects is a three-step process and that's exactly how I organized this chapter. First, you create your Project and add the tasks, milestones, and issues, necessary to complete the project. Then you create project templates to save time in the future. Finally, you track the progress of your Projects.

Zoho Projects can be customized just like any other Zoho application, which means you can add new fields and create layouts. There are four main areas of customization that you can get to through the **Projects Setup icon**:

- Projects
- Tasks

➢ Timesheet

➢ Issues

Zoho Projects includes a sample Project, appropriately called **Explore Zoho Projects!.** Before launching into your own projects, you might want to explore this one a bit to get a better understanding of all the elements that go into Zoho Projects.

As a reminder, Zoho Projects must be purchased separately. It is also included in your Zoho One purchase. You can access Zoho Projects by going to *Projects.zoho.com*.

Creating a Project Is a Major Project

For ages, scholars have debated which comes first: a project or a project template. Project templates are great for duplicating similar projects. However, there are three compelling reasons why it makes sense to create a project first and the template later:

Not all of your Projects may be similar. You'll probably find it beneficial to fully understand Zoho Projects before attempting to create a template. Once you create a successful Project it can be easily transformed into a template.

Here's how to quickly create a new Project:

1. Open **Zoho Projects** and click **Projects** on the **Vertical Navigation** bar. The **Project page** opens.

    Alternatively, you can click the **Projects** tab in **Zoho CRM**.

2. Click the **New Project** button. The **New Project** popup springs to life.

3. Provide a Project Name.

4. (Optional) Choose a template from the **Template** dropdown.

    When you select a template, all the milestones, task lists, tasks, and other information from the chosen project template will be copied to a new project. The start time of the project modules (milestones, task list, and tasks) will be shifted based on the **Project Start Date** of the new project.

5. Select an **Owner** for the project; by default, the owner is YOU.

6. Add the project **Start Date**.

7. (Optional) Select the project **End Date**.

   If you used a template to create the project, you will not see this option.

8. (Optional) Set the **Group Name** and **Tags**.

9. Select the **Budget** for the Project.

   This entails adding the Currency, Project Budget, Billing Method, and Rate Per Hour.

10. (Optional) Check the **Roll-Up** checkbox.

    This option will roll up various activities, including the total of the actual hours logged and the overall project duration based on the task start and end dates, into milestones. Once enabled, you can't disable the roll-up for that project.

11. (Optional) Disable any unwanted tabs in the **Customize Tabs for This Project** area.

    Each project will contain a number of tabs. To simplify things, you may wish to turn off a few of them. For example, you might not add issues to a project, so there is no need to see that tab. Note that the **Dashboard** and **Tasks** tabs can't be turned off, but you can turn a tab back on again if you decide later that you want to access it.

12. Determine whether the access to the project is **Private** or **Public**.

13. Click **Add** to add the project.

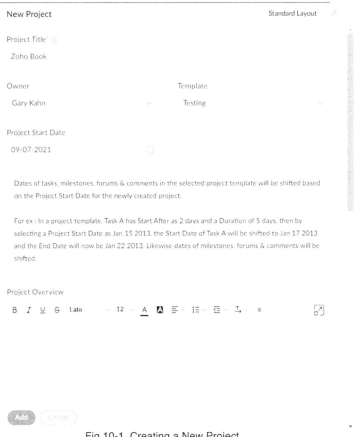

Fig 10-1 Creating a New Project

Your Next Task is to Add a Task

By definition, a project is "a series of tasks that need to be completed in order to reach a specific outcome." A project can also be defined as "a set of inputs and outputs required to achieve a particular goal." Projects can range from simple to complex, and can be managed by one person or a hundred.

Tasks can be added to a Project in a variety of ways:

- Adding tasks manually, one at a time
- Creating a Task List
- Creating a Task List Template
- Using a Project Template that includes tasks

Here's all you need to know to start adding tasks to your projects:

1. Open **Zoho Projects** and click **Projects** on the **Vertical**

Navigation bar. The **Project page** opens. Make sure the **View** dropdown is set to **All Projects**.

2. Click on the name of the Project to which you want to add tasks.

3. Click on the **Tasks** tab.

4. Click the **Add Task** button in the top right corner. The **New Task** popup appears.

5. Enter the **Task Name**.

6. (Optional) Add a **Description.**

7. Set the task **Owner** by choosing a user from the **Select User** dropdown.

    Warning: if you do not assign a Task Owner, the task will not appear on anyone's task list!

8. Enter the other details as necessary.

    You can add as many details to the task as you need including the start and due dates, priority, and the expected duration of the task. If your project has mandatory custom fields, then you must enter data for these fields before you can save the task.

9. Click **Add** to save the task or **Add More** to continue adding tasks.

Fig 10-2 Adding a Task to a Project

Zoho Projects has a funky way of numbering Tasks and Projects. Projects are generally labeled with the first two letters of your company name, followed by numbering in consecutive order. This cannot be changed. However, you can change the prefix used for the tasks themselves by editing the Task & Issue Prefix fields.

Project Speed Tasking

You might be chomping at the bit to get going on your Project. If that's the case, there is another way to add Tasks if you are really in a hurry to get working on your project, but don't need to add much detail. You can only exercise this option after you have created the first task in a project.

1. Open **Zoho Projects** and click **Projects** on the **Vertical Navigation** bar. The **Project page** opens. Make sure the **View** dropdown is set to **All Projects**.

2. Click on the name of the project to which you want to add tasks.

3. Click on the **Tasks** tab. Hover your mouse over the **General** heading and click the **Add Task** hyperlink.

4. Type in the **Task Name** and hit the **Enter** key.

Once you've sped your way through adding multiple tasks, you can go back and edit them to as needed.

Making Milestones out of Molehills

A *Milestone* indicates key events and major forward progress in your project. You might want to think of Milestones as the most important events of your project. You usually reach a Milestone after you have completed a series of Tasks. Without Project Milestones, you're just monitoring Tasks and not necessarily following the right path to completing your project.

To add a Milestone to an existing project:

1. Open **Zoho Projects** and click **Projects** on the **Vertical Navigation** bar. The **Project** page opens. Make sure the **View** dropdown is set to **All Projects**.

2. Select a project from the **Projects** tab in the **Projects Navigation** bar.

3. Click on the **Milestones** tab. The **Milestones** page opens.

4. Click the **Create a Milestone button**. The **New Milestone** popup opens.

5. Give the milestone a name and set its **Start** and **End Dates**.

6. Select an **Owner** for the milestone.

7. Click **Add**.

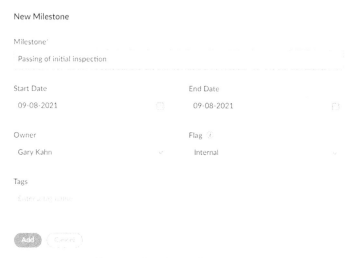

Fig 10-3 Creating a Milestone

Let's Not Make an Issue Out of This

Project issues are anything that come up in the course of your project to impact the plan. Sometimes, the issue can cause your project to grind to a halt and prevent you from successfully completing future tasks. Other times, the issues are ignored or forgotten, and resurface when you least expect them.

It is always good to "expect the unexpected." Good project planning begins with a plan that is able to manage and control issues as they arise during a project. Needless to say, Zoho Projects is more than up to the challenge.

Issues, like just about every other aspect of Zoho Projects, can be further customized. For example, Zoho Projects comes with four issue "severities": Minor, Major, Critical, and Show Stopper. However, not all issues are bad ones; some issues may represent additional opportunities. You can easily modify the **Issue Severity** field by clicking the **Setup** icon, and then choosing **Issues** from the **Layouts and Fields** area. Feel free to modify the severities list to better fit your needs.

To add an issue to a Project:

1. Open **Zoho Projects** and click **Projects** on the **Vertical Navigation** bar. The **Project page** opens.

2. Select a project from the **Projects** tab in the **Projects Navigation** bar.

3. Click on the **Issues** tab and then click the **Submit Issue** button. The **New Issue** popup opens.

4. Enter the **Issue Title**. This is the only mandatory field.

5. Enter other details if necessary.

    You can add a **Description**, attach files, assign the issue to users, set due dates, and add reminders.

6. Click **Add** to save the issue, or **Add More** to continue adding additional issues.

That Was Fun – Let's Do It Again!

Many companies experience a sense of déjà vu when creating projects. For example, swimming pool contractors might find that all their projects require pretty much the same steps in the same order. If you are very lazy - or extremely smart - you might turn to Zoho Projects to create Project and Task List Templates.

Creating Project Templates

When you create a Project Template, you can include the various Project Tasks. You can also assign resources to a Project Template if the same loyal group of folks works on similar projects over and over again. You can then use the saved Project Template to create new Projects. And once created, the Projects you create based on a Template can be edited exactly like any other project.

As you might have already guessed, you can create a new project from scratch, or simply use an existing Project Template. It's only logical to base a project template on an existing project, if you've already gone through the effort of creating one.

To create a project template:

1. Click **Projects** in the **Vertical Navigation Bar** of the **Zoho Projects** app.

2. Change the **View** to **Project Templates**. You will be in the **Project Templates** area.

3. Click the **New Project Template** button. The **Add Project Template** popup opens.

4. (Optional) Select the **Project Layout** that you want to apply to the template if you have created multiple Project layouts.

Remember, you can add custom fields and layouts to the Projects module in the exact same way you do for the Zoho CRM modules. If you haven't created any project layouts, **Standard Layout** is listed at the top of the screen. You can also click the **Pencil** icon if you'd like to modify the existing project layout.

5. Enter the new **Project Template Name**.

6. Select the project that you want to use as a template in the **Choose from Projects** dropdown.

7. **Check** the **Add closed tasks as open tasks** in the project template checkbox.

   The closed tasks in the selected projects will be added as open tasks in the new template. This is your only chance to exercise this option.

8. The remainder of the Project Template details are optional including:

   - ✓ **Project Overview:** Feel free to write a book about the Project if needed.

   - ✓ **Task Layout:** If you have customized the Task layout screen, now's the time to use it.

   - ✓ **Tags:** Dealing with a lot of projects? You can find them easily by creating tags to identify them.

   - ✓ **Budget:** This consists of the Currency you are going to use, and the Project Budget which determines when the customer is billed.

   - ✓ **Billing Method:** In general, Projects are billed on either an hourly or a project basis; feel free to take your pick.

9. Click **Add Project Template** to save your new project template.

I'm Between Projects Right Now

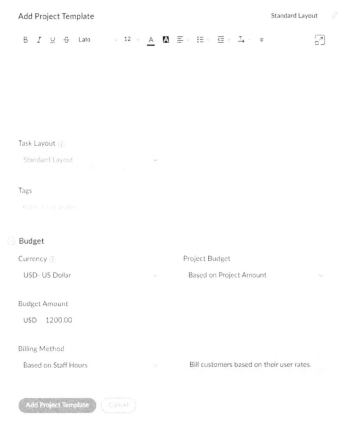

Fig 10.-4 Creating a Project Template

Creating a Project Task List

Zoho Projects has yet another trick up its sleeve: The **Project Task List Template**. This is a quick and easy way for you to add groups of repetitious Tasks to a Project. For example, you might have one set of Tasks for onboarding a commercial client, and another for onboarding a retail client. You might also have one set of installation Tasks for custom items, and another one for your stock items. Using Task List Templates, you can mix and match your various Tasks and add them to a Project.

Here's how to create a Task List Template for your Projects:

1. Click the **Setup** icon in the upper-right corner of the **Zoho Projects** app. The **Projects Setup** page opens.

    Make sure you click the wrench icon that appears under your profile picture and not the gear icon that you use to access the general Zoho preferences.

2. Click **Customization** on the **Vertical Navigation Bar** and select **Task Templates**.

3. Click the **Create a Task List Template** button. The **Create a Task List Template** popup opens.

4. Give the **Task List** a name and then click **Add**. The new task list will appear in the **Task Templates** area of the **Setup** page.

5. Hover your mouse over the new task list name and click the **Add Task** link. The **Add Task** popup opens.

6. Give the task a **Task Name**; this is the only mandatory field.

7. (Optional) Provide the following information:

    - ✓ **Description:** You can add as much information as you need about the task.

    - ✓ **Start After:** Set the time for an interval after the project start date.

    - ✓ **Duration:** Set the estimated time you think it will take to complete the task.

8. Click **Add** to add the task to the **Task List Template**. You will return to the **Task Templates** section of the **Setup** page.

9. (Optional) Repeat steps 5-8 above to add additional tasks to the task template.

10. (Optional) **Hover** your mouse to the left of a task name and click the **Gear** icon to edit, delete, or add a subtask to a task.

11. (Optional) To reorder tasks, **hover** your mouse to the right of the **Task Template** name and click the **Reorder** icon.

I'm Between Projects Right Now

Fig 10- 5 Project Task List

Once you have created a Task List Template it is easy to add it to an existing project by following these steps:

1. Click **Projects** in the **Vertical Navigation Bar** of the **Zoho Projects** app.

2. Change the View to **All Projects**. You will be in the **Project List View**.

3. Select a **Project**; the **Project** will open to the **Tasks** tab.

4. Click the **Add Task dropdown** and select **Add Task List**. The **New Task List** popup opens.

5. Click the **Select from templates** link. The **New Task List** popup opens.

6. Select the appropriate task list from the **Task List** dropdown.

7. Click **Add** to add the **Task List Template** to the current project.

Managing Your Projects

Once you've defined your Project - and created a handful of Project Tasks to help move you along the correct path to your final goal - it's time to kick back and relax, right? Wrong! Creating the Project is only half the fun - now you've got to put your nose to the grindstone and start to work on that Project. Fortunately for you, Zoho is with you every step of the way.

Project Dashboards

Project Dashboards show important progress indicators, graphs, statistics, and other key performance indicators (KPIs), to give you a better understanding as to where a project stands.

You can access dashboards from two areas in Zoho Projects:

- The **Projects Home** page
- The **Dashboard** tab of any specific project

The Project Home page is your project hub. From the Home page you can see a recap of your projects that includes the number of both open and closed Tasks, Issues, and Milestones.

Both the Home page and the Project Dashboard have a number of useful features including:

- Drill down into any of the areas in the Home page with a single click.
- Change the order of the various **Home** page widgets with a simple drag and drop.
- Add or remove widgets by clicking the **More** icon.

The Projects List View

The entire purpose of Zoho Projects is to make sure that you have oversight into the various Milestones in a project, and that you don't overlook any important steps along the way. Viewing the Project List View allows you to easily view key performance indicators (KPIs) in the form of graphs and statistics.

The list view is the view you see when you choose **Projects** from the **Projects Vertical Navigation Bar**. Just like the name indicates, the *Projects List* view lists of all the projects of which you are a part. The Projects List shows you the status of the Project, the number of Tasks completed, the start and end date, planned and actual costs, and budget details. And, as is the case with all Zoho modules, the columns can be customized to show the fields that are most important to you.

The Project List is designed to not only see your Project, but also to make changes to them. Here are a few of the things that you can do in the Projects List:

- Select a different view, or create a new one
- Change Columns
- Sort Columns
- Make changes to the Project's Owner, Status, Start, End, and Complete dates
- Edit a Project
- Delete a Project

- Move a Project to the Archive
- Group your projects
- Add a tag to your projects
- Export Projects

Getting an Overview of Your Work Load

Zoho has multiple places for you to go to check on the status of your various projects.

- **The Project Calendar**: You can filter your calendar, edit an activity or drag and drop an activity to a different date using the Project Calendar.

You can access any of these areas from the **Work Overview** section of the **Projects Vertical Navigation Bar**:

- **Tasks:** Here's where you can get a better handle on all of your project tasks. By default, the tasks display in the Kanban view so that you can easily prioritize your tasks by dragging them from one area to another.
- **Issues:** For many business owners, your day consists of putting out fires; here's where you can go to have a list of all of them in one place.
- **Milestones:** We all sweat the small stuff, but at the end of the day it's important to know when the big stuff is due.
- **Timesheets:** It's only logical that if you devote a lot of time to a project you would like to get paid for it. The Timesheet allows you to track time by project, employee, task or issue, day, and amount of time spent.

Project Reports and Summary Charts

Project management is not easy. You are dealing with multiple projects, multiple tasks and probably multiple headaches. You might also be dealing with multiple employees and multiple clients. You will love the various visual indicators that give you further insights into your projects. However, your clients or contractors might not have access to Zoho and won't be able to make use of the projects' visual clues. Once again, Zoho has your back and includes many useful project reports.

You can easily access the various project reports and dashboards by clicking **Reports** from the **Projects page.** Take a look at the basic reports in the **Project Reports dropdown** that include:

- ➢ **Gantt Chart:** A Gantt chart is a visual representation of the overall status of the project in terms of time and milestones.
- ➢ **Resource Utilization Chart:** This chart helps balance the workloads of your various users.
- ➢ **Planned vs Actual** The Planned vs Actual feature helps you to measure productivity in terms of hours, and understand whether your employees are ahead or behind schedule.

Project Timeline Gantt: View all your project timelines on one Gantt chart. In addition, the **Project Reports dropdown** includes the **Timesheet Reports** which consists of reports for Project and Client-specific Timesheets.

It may seem a bit bizarre, but you can also choose **Project Reports** as an option in the **Project Reports dropdown**. This is where you find another eight Project Reports.Unhappy with the basic Project Reports? You find a number of additional reports, in **Zoho Analytics** which is accessible directly from the **Project Reports dropdown**.

By now you might have reached your fill of reports, but Zoho is not yet finished. You can view six more project-specific reports by accessing the **Gantt & Reports tab** of any project. The project-specific reports include:

- ➢ Gannt Chart
- ➢ Resource Utilization
- ➢ Planned vs Actual
- ➢ Task Report
- ➢ Issue Report
- ➢ Timesheet Report

11

Being Part of a Major Case Squad

In a nutshell, case management is the collaborative process of assessing a problem, planning its solution, and ultimately providing a favorable outcome. In this chapter I show you how to use Zoho's Cases module to identify and fix the problems that are bothering your customers before they snowball into major headaches. And, once you've solved the problem and/or resolved the issues, you can document your findings in the company Knowledge Base.

Fortunately, you may never have to use Zoho's Cases module. Maybe you sell a product that never breaks - or one that you don't have to worry about fixing. Perhaps the services that you offer are so stellar that you never receive a complaint. Lucky you! If that's the case, feel free to skip this chapter.

If your company deals with a lot of product-related issues, Zoho's Cases module may seem heaven-sent. Many other CRM products require you to purchase expensive add-on software to manage a help desk or incident tracking. By having one integrated product, your support personnel can attach the issues to existing records without having to retype address and other contact details in the database.

With Zoho CRM, you can create Cases to deal with a variety of issues and questions that all too often land on your desk. Maybe you sell products or equipment that break. Maybe you run a call center that fields questions about various products. Or maybe your company has a customer service department that needs a place to log the complaints that they have to deal with. Whatever the situation, Zoho is there to handle all negative situations.

State Your Case

Creating Cases and resolving them using Zoho is a very easy process. Creating a Case is much easier than waiting for a small problem to develop into a ton of trouble.

In essence, the customer notifies the help desk, or customer service department, of his or her issue. The support personnel create a case that details the problem. If the first person is able to solve the issue, he can close the case. However, if he is unable to resolve the problem, he can assign a follow-up to someone else in the company who might have better luck in helping Mr. Customer resolve the issue. Needless to say, anyone in the company can view the details of the case from the Cases module.

In addition to reaching out to the customer in question, cases can be used to create reports to give you better insight into which of your products are facing support issues, and identifying the common solutions to those issues.

If your customer service needs are fairly basic, you will probably be quite content with the Cases module found in Zoho CRM. If the Cases module is not exactly to your liking, you can customize the fields in the Cases module in the same way you customize any other module. You can use, edit, or remove any of the existing fields, or add new custom fields if the need arises.

Here's all you need to do to create a case in Zoho CRM:

1. Click **Cases** in the **Horizontal Navigation Bar** to access the **Cases** module.

2. Click **Create Case**. The **Create Case** page opens.

3. Enter the required case details. The more information you add, the better you will be able to resolve the case. Only a few fields are mandatory; you can easily spot them by the red boarder on the left side of the field. Although the **Product Name** and Account Name fields aren't required, they will make the Case visible from the Product and Account modules:

    ✓ **Subject:** Give the Case a title.

    ✓ **Status:** Select the status of the Case from the drop-down list.

    ✓ **Case Origin:** Select the source of the case. You can select **Email, Phone, or Website**. If you select Email, you must specify the **Email ID** of the customer.

- ✓ **Case Owner:** Select the name of the user who will be solving the case. By default, that person is YOU.
- ✓ **Email:** Specify the Email of the contact; this field will only be required if you specified Email as the **Case Origin**.

4. Click **Save** to save the new Case.

A Case Number is automatically assigned once you have finished creating a case. At this juncture, you can add notes or activities to the Case, exactly as you would for Contacts. If you have associated a Case with a Contact, Account or a Deal then you will see the Case listed in the Related List area of the corresponding entity.

When you are ready to close your Case, simply return to the Case and change the Status to **Closed**. It's also a good idea to provide the solution and a comment.

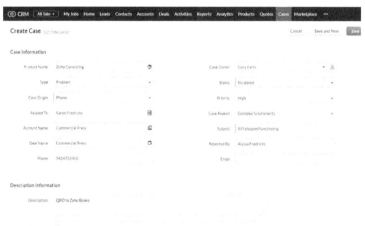

Fig 11-1 Creating a Case

Moving Up to Zoho Desk

In general, the bigger the company, the greater the possibility that things will go wrong. The Cases module is fairly generic so you can use it company-wide to help resolve the issues facing various departments.

If you are part of a company with many moving parts, you may quickly outgrow the Cases module. This is typical in small to medium-sized companies where a ticketing system is used and needs to be visible to a variety of your users. If your needs are more sophisticated, you can add **Zoho Desk** which includes all the functionality you need to run a full-blown customer service ticketing operation. Desk is included with your Zoho One subscription.

In addition to full integration to Zoho CRM, Zoho Desk adds in the following functionality:

- Document Management
- Email Integration
- Social Media Integration
- Customer Portals
- Surveys
- Knowledge Base
- Alerts

One big difference between the CRM Cases and Zoho Desk is the users are called **Agents,** as in Customer Service Agents. In essence, you can transition any of your Users in Zoho One to Agents in Zoho Desk.

I Demand to See Your Complaint Department

If you are using the Desk module, the first thing you may want to set up are your various departments. **Departments** are the various business divisions within your organization. They can be categorized based on your products, geographical locations, or teams. Zoho Desk enables you to create departments and manage customer support individually for each of the divisions within your organization. This allows you to customize a support process independent of your other departments.

As an example, your company might have the need for four separate departments:

- **Customer Service:** The customer service department will use Zoho to keep track of all the issues and problems that your customers report about your products or services.
- **Sales:** Because the entire database is integrated with the customer support issues, your sales folks can see how your customers are being taken care of and what issues they've faced.
- **Marketing:** Marketing can refer to the Desk module to

analyze the nature of problems that your customers are reporting. They can use these insights to improve your products or services.

➢ **Internal IT:** Your overworked and underpaid IT folks can use Zoho to keep track of internal, employee-related tasks so they can prioritize their time.

To add a department:

1. Login to **Desk.Zoho.com**.

2. Click the **Setup** icon in the top right corner of the **Horizontal Navigation Bar**. The **Setup Landing** page opens.

3. Click **Departments** in the **General** section of the **Setup** page. The **Departments** page opens.

4. Click the **New Department** button. The **New Department** page opens.

5. Add the following details:

    ✓ **Department Name:** Provide a name for the department.

    ✓ **Display Name in Help Center:** With Desk, you can create Help Centers for your customers to access. This is the name they will see.

    ✓ **Logo:** Browse and select a logo for the department. The logo is used to identify the department in the Help Center.

    ✓ **Display in Help Center:** Uncheck this option to add a private department if you don't want your customers to have access to this department.

    ✓ **Associate Agents:** There is no end to the sophistication you can achieve in Zoho. You can create "chat agents" to field customer calls, and add those agents to handle the tickets received in this department.

    ✓ **Description**: Enter a description for the department.

6. Click **Configure Channels** which is Desk's way of saying "Save."

Zoho CRM Essentials

Fig 11-2 Creating Departments in Zoho Desk

Let's Make a Federal Case Out of It

In Zoho Desk a *ticket* is equivalent to a Case in Zoho CRM; the main difference is that a ticket has a few more bells and whistles.

To create a **support ticket**:

1. Start a new Support Ticket using one of these options:

    ✓ Click the **Desk** module in Zoho CRM.

    ✓ Go to **Zoho Desk** in the **Related List** area for a Lead, Contact, Account, or Deal record.

    ✓ Go to *Desk.Zoho.com*

Although you can create a ticket in multiple ways, it's logical to start from a record. That way the ticket will be automatically associated with the record.

2. Click the **Plus** icon. The **Add Ticket** page opens.

3. Enter the ticket details.

   The only required fields are the **Contact Name**, the **Subject,** and the **Status**. Don't forget: you can customize Zoho Desk like any other Zoho application. You can add additional fields and require that they be populated when creating a new ticket.

4. (Optional) Click the **Attachment** icon to attach a file to the ticket.

5. Click **Submit**.

Your Tickets appear in the Zoho Desk Related List for any associated records.

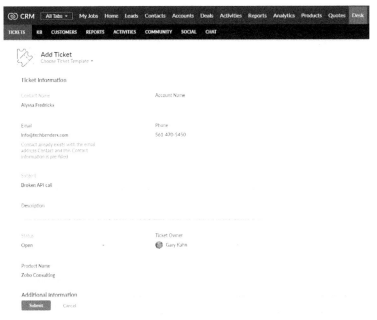

Fig 11-3 Ticket Screenshot

Big Ticket Items

Some tickets have easy resolutions and you can open and close the ticket at the same time. However, many cases are more complex and involve a bit more intervention before they can be closed.

Zoho CRM Essentials

One area that separates Desk from the more vanilla CRM Cases is the tabs that appear along the top of a ticket. When using the Case module, you will see a Timeline tab similar to the one you see in any of the CRM modules. When using Desk, you have access to several tabs in the Desk CRM module including:

- **Conversation:** Here's where you can add a comment and read through the conversations of other agents.
- **Resolution:** This allows you to see if an agent has closed a ticket, and the details as to how a ticket was resolved.
- **Time Entry:** This is where your agents log the time they spend working on each ticket.
- **Attachments:** Any attachments that your agents associate with a ticket will display here.
- **Activity:** You can view any associated tasks, events, and calls here.
- **Approval:** Some companies require an approval to escalate an issue or refund money. Here's where the supervisors can add approval – and your agents can view them.
- **History**: This shows you the ticket's audit trail by displaying all of the activities associated with a ticket.

When working directly from the Desk App you have all the above tabs plus two more:

- **Overview:** Think of this like a dashboard that displays a total for the current number of tickets and overdue tickets, your average happiness rating, and the average response and resolution times.
- **Happiness Rating:** This will display any survey ratings that your customers have submitted.

Building Your Base of Knowledge

The beginning of this chapter deals with the issues that your customers face - and the process you go through to provide a solution. You might think that once the customer goes away - hopefully with a smile on his face - your problems are over. However, chances are pretty good that other customers will be coming to you with the very same issues somewhere down the line. You might start the process all over again - or you might try to learn from your own past experiences.

Zoho Desk includes the ability to create a Knowledge Base. Note that this functionality is only available if you purchase Zoho Desk or Zoho One.

A *knowledge base (also known as KB)* is a collection of articles that pertains to a specific topic. In general, knowledge base articles include a problem and its solution. Typically, a KB includes the ability to search the articles in order to find the answers to your specific questions. The Knowledge Base is where your customers can access the solution articles you create for addressing various issues. You can create articles and group them under custom sections for ease of access.

Creating Knowledge Base Categories

Hopefully over time your Knowledge Base will grow as well. If you want to keep those articles well organized, you will find it useful to assign each article to both a *category* and a *section*.

A category is the main topic. Every KB article must be associated with a category. Each category can be further divided into sections and sub-sections. You can create up to three subsections for each category.

Categories are linked to departments. When you add a new department, it creates a default category in your Knowledge Base. You can add additional sections underneath the category to further organize your articles.

To create KB article categories:

1. Access Zoho Desk by going to *Desk.Zoho.com*.
2. Click **KB** in the Desk **Horizontal Navigation Bar**. The **KB** page opens.
3. Click **Manage KB** on the left **Vertical Navigation Bar**.
4. Click **Organize Categories**. The **Categories** page opens.
5. Click **Create Category** in the top right corner of the page. The **Add Category** window opens on the right.
6. Add the following information on the **Add Category** window:

    ✓ **Display Picture**: You can choose one from the library, or upload a picture from your computer.

- ✓ **Name and Description**.
- ✓ **Departments:** Select the department with which you want to associate the category.
- ✓ **Visibility:** Select a choice from the dropdown to indicate who will be able to access the category. You can choose from **None** (for open access), **Groups, Public, Agents** or **Custom IP.**
- ✓ **Article View:** Specify how you want your customers to read through the articles. With quick navigation, you can group related articles.
- ✓ **Auto-create Tickets from Feedback:** As the name implies, this will automatically create tickets and assign them to the appropriate department and agent.
- ✓ **Reviewers**: Add the users that will be able to publish articles.

7. Click **Save** to save your changes.

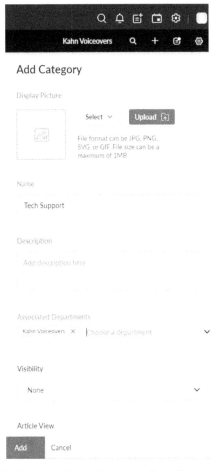

Fig 11-4 Creating a Knowledge Base Category

Sectioning Your Knowledge Base

You can add any number of sections under a category. The sections help you group your articles on a common theme. You can add two more levels of hierarchy to a section.

To add a section in your Knowledge Base:

1. Access Zoho Desk by going to **Desk.Zoho.com**.
2. Click **KB** in the **Desk Horizontal Navigation Bar**. The **KB** page opens.
3. Click Manage **KB** on the **Left Vertical Navigation Bar.**
4. Click **Organize Categories**. The **Categories** page opens.

Zoho CRM Essentials

5. Select the **Category** to which you want to add a section.

6. Click the **Add** link in the **Section** area. The **Add Section** window opens on the right.

    Select a **Display Picture** from the library or upload one from your computer. Give the section a **Name** and **Description**, and then select who will have access to the section from the **Visibility** dropdown.

7. Click **Save** to save your changes. Repeat Step 6 to add more sections or sub-sections.

Fig 11-5 Creating a Knowledge Base Sections

Writing KB Articles

Creating a knowledge base is like writing a book; it requires a lot of time and organization. Luckily for you, if you've followed the previous sections in this chapter, you have created the proper structure of departments, categories, and sections for your articles. Now on to the hard part: writing your articles.

To add your first Knowledge Base article:

1. Access **Zoho Desk** by going to *Desk.Zoho.com.*

2. Click **KB** in the Desk **Horizontal Navigation Bar**. The **KB** page opens.

3. Click the **Plus Sign** and select **Article**. The **Add Article** page opens.

4. Enter article **Title;** this is mandatory in order to save the article.

5. Type the **Solution** in the editor window.
6. (Optional) **Attach** any files that are related to the article.

    You can use **Drag** files from your desktop, **Browse** to select the files you'd like to upload, or click **Gallery** to upload a file from previously saved articles.

7. Select the **Category**, **Section,** and **Sub-section** from the dropdown menus. Needless to say, nothing will appear in the dropdowns if you have not already created them.
8. Set the access **permission**. You can choose to display the article to **Agents**, **All users,** or **Registered users** in the Help Center.
9. Enter relevant **tags**. Tags will be used to display suggested articles for your customers in the Help Center. It will also pull up relevant solutions when your agents respond to **Tickets**.
10. (Optional) Add Tags to the article to make them easy to be found.
11. (Optional) Set an **Article Expiry** date for the article.
12. (Optional) Specify the **Title**, **Meta Description,** and the **Meta Keywords** for the article.

    If you'd like a little extra bang for your buck, adding SEO information will help your article get found by the various search engines.

13. (Optional) Click **Save as Draft** if you would like to revisit the article, or have someone else take a look, before you publish it.
14. Click **Publish** when you are happy with your final product.

Zoho CRM Essentials

Fig 11-6 Creating a Knowledge Base Article

The user or "agent" who creates an article will be its owner. Article owners will be notified of the feedback received from the customers.

Viewing the Fruits of Your Labors

Once you've started entering information into Zoho, you need a way to find it again. You'll want to have a 360 degree view of all your information; you can accomplish this easily by making use of the Home page and dashboards. Other times, you may want to hone in on a single report. Still other times, you might want to access information based on your own very specific criteria. And, once you've found that data, you might even want to print it out for posterity.

I Need a New Home Page

The *Home Page* is the first thing you see when you log into Zoho. The Home Page consists of individual components that summarize your various activities. A component can display a list of records that is similar to the list view displayed on a module's Home Page. You can remove the components that you don't use, modify them so they better suit your needs, or add new ones.

Out of the box you have two Home Page views:

- ➤ Classic
- ➤ Your Own

You switch between these views by clicking on the drop-down menu at the right side of the Home Page.

Getting Classy with the Classic Home Page

The Classic view displays the following three components:

- My Open Tasks
- My Meetings Today
- Amount by Stage

There are very few things you can do to customize the Classic Home Page other than to swap out the My Open Tasks component for a different set of tasks. You can do this by clicking the drop-down to the right of My Open Tasks.

Everyone Wants Their Own Home Page

Each Zoho user has the ability to customize their own Home Page. The home screen can be different for every user. Switching the view from Classic to your own view replaces the My Meetings Today component with the Today's Leads component, and adds the Closing This Month component. It also includes the ability to add, edit, and delete components.

The key to customizing your Home Page is to simply look for the three dots. You'll see them both to the right of each component and at the top right of your Home Page. The ellipsis to the right of the Home Page is where you go to add another component or reorder the existing ones. The individual component ellipsis allows you to delete or edit a component.

There are three sources of components:

- **Dashboards:** I like to think of this as the secret goodies stash, as Zoho has created dozens of great dashboards that you can easily add to your Home Page.
- **Custom Views:** These are based on the Custom List Views that you have created for each module.
- **Widgets:** These are customized components created by someone at your company with either good software development skills – or the money to pay for someone with good software development skills.

Building Your Own Home Page

If you are an Administrator, you can customize the Home Page for other users based on what you want them to look when they log into Zoho CRM. When you customize a Home Page you can share it with specific users based on their assigned Role. Users can switch

Viewing the Fruits of Your Labors

between any of the Homepage views that are available to them.

To begin customizing the Home Page:

1. Click the drop-down on the top right corner of the **Home Page** and select **Customize Home** page. Alternatively, you can click the **Setup** icon and then choose the **Customize Home** page option in the Customization area. In either case, the **Customize Home** page opens.
2. Click the **New Home Page** button. The **Untitled Home Page** opens.
3. Click **Dashboard** on the left side of the **Home Page**.
4. Choose a **Dashboard** from the dropdown list and then select the specific **Components** that you want to add to the Home Page.
5. Click **Custom View**.
6. Choose a **Module** from the dropdown list and then select the **Component** you want to add.

    The sky is the limit and there are dozens of components from which to choose.

    Feel free to add components to your Home Page until you are happy with the final results. The components that you add in the Home tab can take the form of a list view, or data, in the form of a pipeline, pie chart, or bar graph. When adding List View components, you can easily add, delete, and reorder the columns using the same methodology you used when customizing the tabular view for any module.

7. Drag the various components around the **Home Page** until you like and are comfortable with their arrangement. The grid lines will make it easy for you to line up the components.
8. **Resize** and rearrange the components to further organize the page once all the required components are added.

    The Custom View components tend to be wider than the Dashboard components. However, you can easily change this by clicking on a component and changing the size by grabbing the selection handles.

9. Click the **Save & Share** button. The **Edit Properties** window opens.

10. Make the following changes in the **Edit Properties** window:

   ✓ Specify a **name** for the customized Home Page.

   ✓ Choose the **roles** of the users with which you want to share the Home Page.

11. (Optional) Add a **description**.

12. Click **Save** to save your new **Home Page**.

Fig 12-1 Creating a New Homepage

Once created, users are not able to edit the Home Page unless they are Administrators and have the permission to edit the Setup area.

Tabbing Through Your Tabs

The main horizontal menu in Zoho CRM contains links to each of the Modules. We refer to those menu links as Tabs. By default, there are 18 Modules or Tabs, each representing a different set of functions or subset of data. You can customize these Tabs according to your needs. Organizing Tabs allows you to display the Modules you need and hide the rest. For example, you might use other software to create Quotes and Invoices, so these Modules can be hidden. You can also change the order of the Modules.

Tab Group settings are company-wide and only users with administrator privileges can customize them. You can also create **Tab Groups** that contain specific modules for your users. The Tab Group is normally associated with a user's profile permissions. For example, your sales department might need the Quotes and Invoices tab, whereas the customer service department would only need to view the Cases module. You can create up to 25 tab groups, and each tab group can contain an unlimited number of tabs.

To create a tab group:

1. Click the **Setup Gear**. The **Setup** page opens.
2. Click **Modules and Fields** in the **Customization** area. You will be on the **Modules** tab.
3. Click the **Tab Groups** tab and then click the **New Tab Group** button. The **Tab Groups** window opens.
4. Check the **modules** that you want to display.
5. Select the **Permissions** that the Tab Group applies to.
6. Click **Save** to save the Tab Group.

Users can access the Tab Group by selecting the drop-down to the right of the CRM logo.

Working with Reports

After you build your database, the fun part is digging in and using it. Remember, the information that you can pull out of a database is only as good as the information you put into it.

Zoho comes with dozens of reports right out of the box. Whether you run and view your reports online, or if you want to go old-school and print your reports, chances are good that one of the basic reports will give you the information that you're looking. And yes, you can modify, duplicate, and save any of the Zoho CRM reports. If you need something beyond what is baked in, you can create your very own shiny new report, or if you are really feeling ambitious, you might take a look at Zoho Analytics to take your reporting out of the stratosphere.

Types of Reports

Zoho has three types of reports:

- **Tabular Report:** These reports do not include any subtotals in the report. Use this type of report to create contact mailing lists, or a basic sales pipeline that doesn't require totals. The *Potentials Closing by this Month* is a good example of a Tabular Report.
- **Summary Report:** This is probably the most common report type as it displays the data along with subtotals, groupings, and other summary information. An example of this is the *Pipeline by Stage* report.

> **Matrix Report:** Displays the data in a grid using both horizontal and vertical columns. An example of this is the *Stage vs Potential Type* report.

Running and Customizing Existing Reports

Considering how powerful a report can be, it is ridiculously easy to run one:

1. Click the **Reports** tab. The **Reports** page opens.
2. Select the **folder** that contains the desired report from the folder list on the left side of the **Reports** page.
3. Click on the name of the report you want to run. It will open up.

Once the report opens, you see several options based on the report you are running:

> **Filters:** Here's where you can change the date-based criteria for a report.

> **Export:** You can export a file to Excel or PDF format.

> **Send Email:** Share the report with your closest friends.

> **Edit:** This option is actually two in one: Edit and Duplicate. Proceed with caution.
>
> Once you customize and save a report, you cannot revert to the default report. Rather than changing a report and having to live with the changes later, consider duplicating the report – just in case!

> **Create Chart:** As the saying goes, a picture can definitely be worth a thousand words. These charts can be saved as Dashboards and used as Components on your Home Page!

Fig 12-2 Viewing a Report

Creating New Reports

You will be as happy as a clam with the reports that come with Zoho. Or, by duplicating an existing report and tweaking it slightly, you might find that you have exactly the information that fits your situation or need. However, if the existing reports are not displaying the information you need you can create reports from scratch.

Prior to creating a new report, you should probably do a bit of homework and set the parameters in advance. Every report has five elements:

- The **Module** and the corresponding **Cross-Functional Modules.** You can include up to three modules per report.
- The **Report Type** (Tabular, Summary, or Matrix)
- The **Columns** which show how your fields are grouped and if they are totaled. Remember, the columns represent the fields in your database.
- The **Filters** and **Advanced Filters** that determine which records will appear in the report.
- A **Name** and a **Folder** location.

Creating a report is relatively easy once you've done your homework:

1. Click the **Reports** tab on the **Horizontal Navigation Bar**. The Reports Home page opens.

2. Click **Create Report** in the Reports Home page. The **New Report** page opens.

3. Select the primary module from the drop-down list.

4. Select the cross-functional modules from the **Select Related Modules** box and click **Continue**. You can select up to two related modules.

   The modules you select will be used to define criteria, add columns in your report, and select columns to total.

5. Select the **Report Type** and click **Continue**.

   Each time you click Continue, the New Report page expands. This makes it easy to view or change your previous options.

6. Scroll down the **Available Columns:** list and select the report columns.

   This is where you can add any of the existing fields as **Columns to your report**. If you don't see a specific column, it may reside in a module outside of what you have selected. A good example is, if you want to include the Account name in a Contact report, you need to include the Account Module.

7. (Optional) Change the order of the report columns in the **Selected Columns:** area.

8. (Optional) Click the **Grouping** tab. The **Grouping** tab is only available if you are creating a Summary Report.

   Zoho displays the columns that you selected when creating the report. You can select up to three fields and select **Ascending** or **Descending** to determine how the line items in your report are grouped.

9. (Optional) Click the **Columns to Total** tab and choose the fields to include in the report's calculations, then click **Continue**.

   From the list of the numeric fields included in your report, you can choose to display the Sum, Average, Lowest Value, or the Largest Value for any of the fields you select. You can include a Record Count for the line items in your report.

10. Add **filters** to your report to hone in on exactly the data you would like to see in your report.

    As an example, you might only want to report on new leads that are in the state of New York, or notes that were added within the last 30 days.

11. Once you complete the report customization, do one of the following:

    - ✓ **Run:** This option displays a preview of your report. Happy with the results? Click Save. Need to return to the drawing board? Click Edit.
    - ✓ **Save:** This option saves your report. You can also save from a preview of your report.
    - ✓ **Cancel:** Proceed with caution. This option sends you back to Ground Zero!

12. In the **Save Report** popup window, specify the **Report**

Viewing the Fruits of Your Labors

Folder, the **Report Name**, and an optional **Description** of the report.

13. Click **Save**.

Fig 12-3 Creating a Report

Scheduling Reports

Having a myriad of reports at your disposal is only half the battle. The other half comes from actually running them and having them land with a loud plop on the appropriate person's desk. For example, you could train all of your sales people on how to run reports, and chase them around every Monday morning to make sure they actually do it. Or you could wave the white flag, rely on a bit of Zoho magic, and have the reports run automatically.

Here's how you setup the Report Scheduler

1. Click the **Reports tab** on the Horizontal Navigation Bar.
2. Click **Scheduled Reports** in the **Reports Home** page.
3. Click **New Report Schedule**.

4. Specify the Basic Information in the **New Report Scheduler** page.

   Here's where you indicate the Report to schedule, a start date, and how often to send the report.

12. Indicate the **Recipients**.

    Zoho can send the report to anyone in your organization, as well as to various other friends and family who might not work for you.

13. Click **Schedule**.

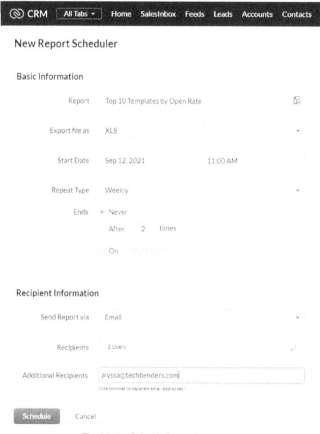

Fig 12-4 . Scheduling a Report

Showing a Bit of Favoritism

With the all the reports that Zoho has to offer, you'll probably want to earmark a few of them to avoid searching for them again next time. This is such a simple thing and yet is such a timesaver!

1. Click the **Reports tab** on the Horizontal Navigation Bar. The Reports page opens.
2. Click the **folder** that contains one of your favorite reports.
3. Click the **Star** to the left of the report name.

Your report will now appear in the Favorite Reports folder. Want to remove it from your favorites? Simply deselect it by clicking on the star.

Organizing Your Reports

With over 70 reports – and more being added all the time – you need to organize your reports. Zoho automatically organizes existing reports into folders to make reports easy to find. However, you can easily change this structure to better serve your needs.

- **Favorite Reports:** This is where reports that you have marked as Favorites appear.
- **Recent Reports:** This shows the last 25 reports that you have run.
- **Reports Created by Me:** This is where you find all your shiny new reports.
- **Shared Reports:** Not sure who can access your creations? Find out here!
- **Scheduled Reports:** This gives you a list of all your scheduled reports in case you need to stop or modify a scheduled report.

In addition, you have a lot of additional leeway as to how you would like to organize your reports including:

- **Reordering Categories:** Click the **gear icon** to the right of any report folder and select **Reorder**. You can move the folders around – or remove folders that you don't need.
- **Renaming a Report Folder:** Click the **gear icon** to the right of any report folder and select **Edit**.
- **Moving Reports to a Different Folder**.
- **Create a Custom Reports Folder:** Select a report, click the **Move to Folder** dropdown, and select Create Folder.

Dashing Through the Dashboards

Zoho comes complete with mag wheels and enhanced dashboard functionality. A **Dashboard** is a visual snapshot of a part of your business. Dashboards can take the form of a neat graphical chart; others come in the form of a list. You might think of this as an SAT analogy: Reports are to Words as Dashboards are to Pictures. You can create a dashboard and share it with all users, or just a few select users. You can also create private dashboards that are accessible only to you and the guys that write the paychecks.

A Dashboard consists of **components**. Each component reflects information that is specific to a portion of your data. Each component displays information differently, allows different actions, and allows you to drill down into the specific data referenced in the component.

The hardest part about using Dashboards in Zoho might be finding where they are in your version of Zoho. That's because Dashboards are part of Zoho Analytics. If you are new to Zoho, the Analytics page will be limited to Dashboards. However, if you are using Zoho One and have already connected Zoho Analytics to other Zoho apps, you will find many more options on the Analytics page and will have to select Dashboard from the vertical Navigation bar.

Before creating new dashboards it's a good idea to peruse the existing ones. Really like one of the dashboards? There are several ways to get back to it easily. Simply click on the three dots to the right of a dashboard, and choose one of these options:

- Print
- Add to Home (as in your Home Page)
- Embed URL
- Add as Favorite

Do you like, but not love, a dashboard? Again, those three little dots allow you to Clone or Edit a dashboard.

Creating a Component from a Report – and Add It to A Dashboard

Once you've had time to check out all Dashboards that come with Zoho, you might feel compelled to start creating new Dashboards. Rather than creating new dashboard components, you might prefer to leverage an existing report. Zoho makes it super easy to create a Dashboard component directly from most reports. As if that

Viewing the Fruits of Your Labors

wasn't impressive enough, you can add most reports to an existing Dashboard at the click of a button.

Here's all you need to know:

1. Click the **Reports** tab on the **Horizontal Navigation Bar**. The **Reports** page opens.

2. Select the **folder** that contains the desired report from the folder list on the left side of the **Reports** page.

3. Select a **Report**. Zoho displays the report.

4. Click **Create Chart** in the top right corner of the report.

5. Select a **Chart Type**.

6. (Optional) Change the field that determines the **X-axis** and **Y-Axis**.

7. Click **Save**. The chart appears.

8. Click the **Chart Options** button in the top right corner, and then click **Add to Dashboard**. The **Add As Dashboard Component** popup window appears.

9. Select the **Dashboard** to which you would like to add the Chart.

10. (Optional) Change the **Component Name** to better reflect the name of the new chart, and then click **Add**.

Fig 12-5 Creating a Dashboard Component

Creating New Dashboards

At times it seems like the options for customizing a Zoho database is endless. Once you've familiarized yourself with the existing Zoho Dashboards you might want to attempt to create one "from scratch." As you might have guessed, you can create your own custom dashboards with little or no programming experience.

1. Click the **Analytics** tab on the Horizontal Navigation Bar. The **Dashboard** page opens.
2. Click the **Add** icon in the top left corner of the **Dashboard Builder** page. The **Dashboard Editor** opens.
3. Fill in a **Dashboard Name**.
4. Select the **users** with whom you want to share the dashboard. You have a choice of:

    ✓ **Only me**: Accessible only to you.

    ✓ **All users**: Shared to all users in your CRM.

    ✓ **Custom:** Select users from different sources like list of users, roles & subordinates or groups.

5. **Click** on a **component** from the left-hand side of the **Editor**.

    At this juncture you might want to call in a Wall Street analyst because you have numerous components that you can add to your dashboard. Not to worry, as you click each component you will be able to see sample data. The Component types include:

    ✓ **Chart:** Chart is a graphical representation of your data. It gives a quick insight of the records for an easy analysis.

    ✓ **KPI:** Lets you measure the performance of your team.

    ✓ **Comparator:** Gives you a comparative overview of any data including user performance, lead source etc.

    ✓ **Anomaly Detector:** Detects any type of discrepancy in your usual business process.

    ✓ **Target Meter:** Lets you set and monitor targets for your team.

    ✓ **Funnel:** Provides you a visual depiction of different stages in your business.

Viewing the Fruits of Your Labors

- ✓ **Cohort:** Time-based data derived from a pattern or change that happens weekly, monthly, yearly, or quarterly.

- ✓ **Quadrant**: Scatters the data that you want to analyze or measure into four quadrants.

6. Select a **Component Style**, provide a **Component Name**, select your options, and Click **Done**. The new component will now appear on your new Dashboard.

7. (Optional) Click the **Pick from Gallery** component to select a pre-existing component.

8. **Repeat steps 5 through 7** until you are finished adding components.

9. (Optional) Click on a Component and **drag the fill handles** to resize it.

10. (Optional) Drag a Component to a different location on the dashboard to rearrange the components.

11. Click **Save** to retain your new dashboard when you're finished.

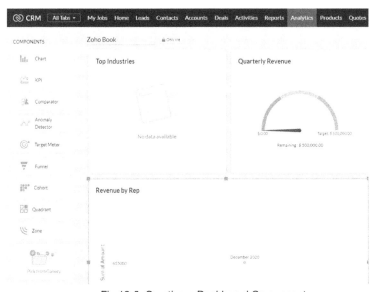

Fig 12-6 Creating a Dashboard Component

13

ZohoPaloozza: Hacks & Shortcuts

As much information as this book contains, you might feel that it has barely skimmed the surface. You may be correct. There is a lot that you can do with Zoho. In this chapter, you'll find a bunch of Zoho features that can make your life a whole lot easier, and your business a lot more efficient!

Add an Attachment to a Record

A great CRM system like Zoho is an excellent way to wrangle the pandemonium that resides on your desk. Using attachments is a good way to do this. Some documents such as Quotes and Invoices are already easily accessible, and you may also want to access things like contracts or even photos that relate to an installation.

Here's how to attach a file:

1. **Navigate** to the record to which you would like to attach a document. Attachments can be added to any module except for Dashboards, Reports, and Forecasts.

2. Click the **Plus** icon next to **Attachments** in the **Related List area.** The **Attach File** popup window opens.

3. Select the location of the file. Zoho makes this easy to do and you can associate a record to a document that resides in any one of these places:

    ✓ **Upload File:** Your own computer's hard drive

    ✓ **Documents:** The Documents section of CRM

    ✓ **Zoho WorkDrive:** Zoho's shared document

application
- ✓ **Zoho Docs:** Zoho's older shared document application
- ✓ **Google Docs**
- ✓ **A Link (URL)**

4. **Navigate** to the location of the file or paste in the URL. You can attach up to five files at one time.
5. Click **Attach.** The attached files will be available in the Attachments section.

Another cool way to add an attachment directly to Zoho is from an incoming or outgoing email attachment. Simply scroll to the bottom of the email and click the **Add to Attachments Related List**. This timesaver requires that you have your email integrated with Zoho CRM.

The Zoho Sheet View

There are times when you need to get a lot of data into Zoho – but you don't have an overabundance of time. Or maybe you need to update a whole bunch of records but don't have the patience to go through your records one by one and change them. If this sounds familiar, you will love the Zoho Sheet view.

The Zoho Sheet View option lists records of a module in a Zoho Sheet spreadsheet. Using the Sheet View, you can view all the records, make necessary changes, and save the sheet. Once saved, the records will automatically update back to Zoho CRM. Alternatively, you can add new records to the sheet and these records will be added to Zoho CRM.

Just a bit of warning; as wonderful as you might find the Zoho Sheet View, it does have a few annoying restrictions:

- ➢ The record ID column is very important, and will appear as Column A in Zoho Sheet. Do not change or modify it.
- ➢ Records will be updated or added to Zoho *only* after you save the sheet.
- ➢ You can push a maximum of 100 records to Zoho Sheet View that you can then edit; however, you can add more rows to an open sheet and they will import back to your database.
- ➢ You cannot delete records using Zoho Sheet.

- ➢ Zoho Sheet view is not available for Activities, Forecasts and Accounting modules.
- ➢ Make sure that your desired field names are displayed in the module list view before moving to Sheet View. New Columns added to Sheet view are not written back to Zoho CRM.

Here's how you can save yourself a bunch of time with Sheet View:

1. Go to the **module** to which you'd like to add records or make changes.
2. **Select** or create a **View**; it doesn't matter how many records are in your view as only 100 of them end up in Zoho Sheet.
3. **Change** the **column headings** as needed. For example, if you only want to update expiration dates, include the Expiration Date field. Also include another identifier such as the name of the person or company.
4. **Click** the **ellipses** in the top right and select **Zoho Sheet View**.
5. **Make** your **changes** or add new records. Ensure that any new data you add is properly aligned with the Column Headings, this writes back to the field level data.
6. Click **Save** – and be patient! The Sheet is saved once you see **Spreadsheet Saved Successfully** flash across the top middle area of the Sheet.
7. **Close** the **Sheet**. And again, **be patient**! You may need to refresh your screen to see all of your changes.

Exporting Records

There are a number of reasons to export a list of your records. You might need to give a list of your contacts to a mailing house in order for them to send out those slick new brochures they've created for you. Or maybe you want to share a list of the Contacts with a non-Zoho user.

Although there are several ways to export your data from Zoho CRM, there are a few best practices to ensure you get what you intend.

Your options include:

➢ Use **Zoho Sheet View**: Unfortunately, this only allows you to export 100 records at a time.

➢ Use the **Export utility** in the Setup area: You can export 3,000 records at a time, but unfortunately you can't query which 3,000 records get exported.

➢ **Export from a report**: If exporting to Excel, you are limited to 2,000 records, but at least you can customize the report to include the exact records you would like to include. You can export up to 20,000 records if you choose CSV file format.

So, what are you to do if you need to export more than 20,000 records at one time? There's actually a simple solution: get a backup of your data. The Zoho CRM backup consists of a handy dandy zip file that contains separate files for each of your Zoho modules in .csv format. Best of all, you will see all records for each module.

Analyzing Things with Zoho Analytics

According to Zoho's marketing materials, Zoho Analytics is a "self-service BI and data analytics software that lets you visually analyze your data, create stunning data visualizations, and discover hidden insights in minutes." A simpler way to state this is by saying that this is the place where you can go to access even more reports, as well as to create a few of your own from scratch.

Analytics comes in a few flavors. Advanced Analytics for Zoho CRM will appear as a tab in Zoho CRM so that you can easily access all of the additional Analytics reports and dashboards for your CRM data. You can also upgrade to the Analytics app which you can either purchase, or is included if you have Zoho One. The Analytics app provides you with dozens of additional reports and dashboards across the entire gamut of Zoho products. And, if you are clever – or at least good at understanding data – you can create additional reports on your own. You can even add in external sources of data from other sources, ranging from Facebook and Mail Chimp to QuickBooks and Spotify.

We're Off to See the Wizard

The Wizard feature helps you divide a long form into a series of screens, where users can enter data on each successive screen until they have entered all of the necessary data to complete the creation of a record. If your sales people have the attention span of a flea, you might find Wizards helpful. A step-wise approach is less overwhelming and reduces chances of erroneous data entry, as the partially completed form can be saved as a draft and completed later.

A Wizard consists of one or more entry forms tied together by a button. Each button takes you to the next form. If you do not go through all of the forms in the Wizard, the record is saved as a Draft record. The final form in the Wizard contains a button that allows you to save the record in its entirety.

To create a data entry form:

1. Click the **Setup Gear**. The **Setup** page opens.
2. Click **Wizards** in the **Customization** area. The **Wizards** page will open.
3. Click **Create Wizard**. The **Create a wizard** popup appears.
4. Enter the **Wizard Name**, select a **Module** from the drop-down list, and choose the **Layouts** the Wizard will apply to.
5. Click **Next** to continue. The **Design** page opens.
6. **Double Click the link to create a screen** button. The **Wizard Design Builder** will open.

    If you might think this step is a bit counter-intuitive, you are not alone in your thinking.

7. In the **Wizard Design** page do the following:

    ✓ Enter the **Screen name**.

    ✓ Enter the **Segment Title**.

    ✓ Drag and drop the required fields into the segment from the **Fields** tab on the left-hand side.

8. Click the Button link. The **Button** popup will slide open.
9. **Name** the button.

    If this is the first button, you can give it a catchy name like **Next**, **Click to Continue,** or even describe the upcoming field. If this is the final button in your wizard, click the, **Use this button to save the record** checkbox.

10. Click **Done**. You will be redirected to the main design page, where you can add edit the segment, or add more segments by double-clicking the existing segment, and returning to the **Wizard Design Builder**.

11. Click the existing button and then click the **Link to screen** hyperlink.

    This will return you to the **Main Design** page which will now contain an additional screen.

12. Double-click the second screen to open the **Wizard Design Builder**.

13. Repeat Steps 7 through 11 until you have finished adding all of the input screens you need.

14. Click **Save Wizard** to save the Wizard.

If your Wizard is missing a key field, or you neglected to create an action for one of the buttons, Zoho will prompt you to try again by filling in the missing elements.

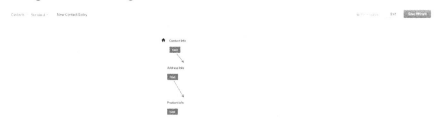

Fig 13-1 Creating a Wizard

Creating a Webform

For some people, adding Leads to a database involves copy and pasting from an email received from your website's Contact Us form. This is likely not your definition of a fun time. With Zoho CRM Webforms, you can easily automate this process.. As its name implies, a **web form** is a *form* on a web age that lets visitors enter their contact information. Zoho Webforms have two big benefits:

- No HTML is required.
- Zoho CRM Webforms are **responsive**, which means they adjust automatically to the screen size, browser, or mobile device, on which they are being viewed.
- The information is automatically captured and added to your database.

One of the best things about Zoho CRM Webforms is how easy they are to setup. Here's all you need to do to create one:

1. Click the **Setup Gear**. The **Setup** page opens.

2. Click **Webforms** in the **Developer Space** area. The **Webforms** tab will open.

3. Choose the appropriate **module** from the drop-down list.

   You can create Webforms for the Leads, Contacts, Cases, and your custom modules. Any existing Webforms for the selected module are listed.

4. Click the **New Form** button. The **New Form** popup window pops up.

5. Enter the **Form Name** and change the **Module** name if needed in the New Form popup.

6. Click **Create**. The **Webform Builder** opens.

7. **Drag** the desired fields from the left Navigation Bar to the form. The available fields from your selected module display down the left side of your screen. The object of the game is to drag and drop the fields you want your web visitor to fill out, onto the Webform Builder. You'll notice that any mandatory fields already appear on the form.

8. (Optional) **Hover** your mouse on the right edge of any field to **remove** it.

9. (Optional) **Hover** your mouse on the right edge of any field and click the **Gear** icon to open the **Field Properties** popup.

   This is where you can change the label of your fields. This doesn't affect the CRM field name; it simply displays a more customer-facing, friendly label. You can also, mark a field as required, add a hint message or a help link to a field, or mark a field as a hidden field. As an example, you might want to identify all leads coming in from your blog. You might add the Lead Source field, mark it as hidden, and enter Blog as the default value.

10. (Optional) Click **Advanced fields** from the **Left Navigation Bar**.

    This is where you can add your privacy policy, a space for visitors to upload a file, or add a captcha to prevent spam.

11. Set the font and layout attributes of the form from the **Formatting Toolbar**.

12. (Optional) Click the **Preview** button to take a look at your final product.

13. Click **Next** to continue.

    Add other details about the webform. The only ones that are mandatory are the location the form will be added to, and the page that visitors should see once they submit the form.

14. Click **Save** to save your web form.

Fig 13-2 Creating a Web Form

At this point, you are served the code required to add your new Webform to your website in a couple different formats – Source, Embed, or iFrame. Check with your web developer if you aren't certain which applies to your site.

Send a Survey

With Zoho Survey you can create an unlimited number of online surveys for free. Yes, you read correctly. Even the free version of Zoho Survey allows you to send an unlimited number of surveys. The only caveat is that the free edition limits the number of questions and the number of responses.

Zoho Survey includes over 250 pre-designed templates in the following categories:

- Customer Satisfaction
- Marketing
- Human Resources
- Events
- Business

Needless to say, you can easily modify any of the templates to better reflect your brand. Or, if you are so inclined, you can easily build a new Survey following these steps:

1. Go to *Survey.Zoho.com*

2. Select one of the **Survey categories** or click the **Create Survey from Scratch** link. The **Survey** page opens.

   You'll have plenty of time later on down the road to explore the numerous survey templates; for now, we are going to concentrate on building one from scratch.

3. Fill in the **Survey Name** field, an optional **Category** and then click **Create**. The **Survey Builder** opens.

   The Survey Builder contains over 25 question types in the Navigation Bar running down the right side of the screen. Drag the corresponding question type onto the builder page. As you drag the various elements on to the page, popup windows open, asking you for additional information. For example, if you want to add a **Short Answer** question, provide a question and indicate if the question is mandatory. Other question types, such as **Multiple Choice** and **Dropdown**, require you to supply both the question and the answers.

4. (Optional) Click the **Plus** icon to add additional pages to your survey.

5. (Optional) Click **Preview** to take a look at the survey.

6. Click the **Launch** tab when you are finished with your survey, and then click the **Publish** button.

   You will see the link that you can either imbed, in your website, or send out via email.

Once you have transmitted your survey, you can view the responses in the Reports area. Short and Long Answer questions include a Sentiment Analysis that analyzes the written responses based on various keywords.

To sign up for Zoho Survey go **TechBenders.com/Survey**.

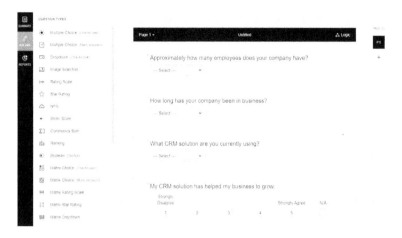

Fig 13-3 Creating a Zoho Survey

Route it with RouteIQ

Tired of spending hours planning delivery, service, or sales routes? Then check out RouteIQ which creates optimized routes automatically.

RouteIQ is a relatively new Zoho app, but it contains several valuable features:

> ➢ Plan a route which is automatically optimized based on the distance, appointments, and drop-ins.
> ➢ Adjust the route as you go if there are any cancellations or new customers to add.
> ➢ Single-click navigation to any customers or any planned routes.

Because RouteIQ requires that your data will be shared with Google Maps and that you install an app, you need to agree to Zoho's Terms of Service to use this feature. You can do so at *Routeiq.Zoho.com*.

RouteIQ is free for your first 1,000 contacts, after which there is an associated fee. The best way to avoid overages is to create a View of your contacts so that only the pertinent portion of your database will be mapped in RouteIQ.

Once RouteIQ is installed and configured, it appears as a tab in Zoho CRM. To create a service route, simply add the route beginning and end points, and start to add contacts. RouteIQ automatically creates a route on the map that you can easily adjust to reflect the most logical order. To create a sales route, add a location and RouteIQ displays all of your Contacts in that area.

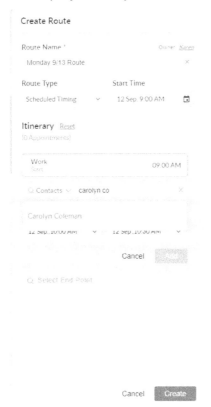

Fig 13-4 Creating a Route

Sometimes You Just Cliq with Someone

Zoho Cliq is a real-time messaging system that can be used for contacting people both from inside and outside of your organization.

You may be familiar with Slack, a software app that lets you chat securely with co-workers and contacts. I laughed when I read that another CRM product paid over 27 billion dollars to acquire Slack because Zoho already has a comparable product, Cliq. In fact, if you use Slack, you can migrate your system over to Cliq.

The cool thing about Cliq is that you can access it either directly from the Cliq site at *cliq.zoho.com,* or from the status bar at the bottom of your CRM product. Cliq can be used with contacts both inside your organization as well as contacts outside your organization. Invites must be sent to users, and once accepted at the other end, they will become your contacts. Within your organization, you can talk and collaborate with users who are not your contacts (status won't be viewable); whereas External users must be your contact in order to establish a connection with them.

Follow these steps to setup the Zoho Cliq integration to Zoho CRM:

1. Click the **Setup Gear**. The **Setup** page opens.
2. Click **Zoho** in the **Marketplace** area. The **Zoho** page will open.
3. Click the **Setup now** button adjacent to **Cliq** section.
4. Click **Enable**.

   When you return to CRM, click the **Smart Chat** area at the bottom of the screen. This is where you can easily create new Channels and invite additional contacts to Cliq.

5. Click on the **Contacts** icon on the bottom **Status Bar**.
6. Type the **email address** of the contact that is associated with a Zoho account in the **Search Contacts** area.

   In order to invite someone to your Cliq network, they must either use Zoho or Cliq.

7. (Optional) Click **Add to your contacts**.

   If you are trying to invite a member of your own company, they must have a Contact record in your Zoho database. If not, you will be prompted to add them as a contact.

8. Click **Invite user to Contacts.**

The contact will receive the invite on their own Cliq screen and via email. If the user does not have a Zoho Cliq account, they will receive an email to sign-up.

ZohoPaloozza: Hacks & Shortcuts

Fig 13-5 Smart Chat

14

I'd Like to Start with an App

This book is primarily about Zoho CRM, the core product in the Zoho product line. It also covered a few of the more popular products including Zoho Desk and Zoho Products. And you've learned how these features work using a standard web browser. However, one of the keys to the Zoho success story is how easy it is to access your data across devices. Whether you spend most of the day on the road, or just like to take a peek at something while relaxing in front of the tube, Zoho has a way to keep you connected. Virtually all of the elements in this book have a corresponding mobile app.

Zoho One

Zoho is probably best known for its CRM functionality. However, in recent years this functionality has expanded to include 45 applications and the number is growing rapidly. Zoho offers most of their apps via bundles like **Zoho One**. These tools are so comprehensive that some people refer to Zoho One as the "operating system for business." If you use the Zoho One, you can run your entire business without ever having to install a single piece of software. Imagine that!

You might think of Zoho One as an "all-you-can-eat" buffet of software. My rule of thumb is that if you use two or more of the Zoho applications, it is less expensive to purchase Zoho One than it would be to pay for each of the apps individually.

Zoho One has an amazing array of functionality. Think of a typical day. A new lead fills out a form on your website; you need to get the contact into your database immediately and then give him a one-on-one demo. After that, you might send a quote, which the prospect hopefully approves so that the quote converts to an invoice. You then receive a payment which is recorded in your accounting system. Of course, you'll want to modify the contact and categorize him as a customer rather than a prospect.

Wouldn't it be nice if all these processes were **automated**? And that all these processes were **integrated**? That's the beauty of Zoho One.

You might die of boredom – and my fingers would grow numb – if I listed all of the Zoho One apps. Besides that, new apps are being added to Zoho One on a fairly routine basis and quite frankly I haven't tried every single one. However, here's a list of the areas covered by Zoho One:

- **Sales:** For the most part, this includes CRM, the Zoho One flagship product, as well as its baby siblings Bigin and Contact Manager. Zoho Bookings is an online scheduling system that lets contacts schedule appointments, or enroll in classes.

- **Marketing:** Zoho's Marketing Suite includes digital marketing tools to help engage your business with the outside world. Zoho Marketing apps include Zoho Sites, a simple website builder, and Zoho Social, a platform that automates your social marketing. And of course, marketing isn't marketing without a bit of Marketing Automation and Campaigns.

- **Support:** If you sell a product you may have to support it as well; Zoho Desk and Zoho Assist provide you with the ability to create, track, automatically assign support tickets, and access your customer's computer remotely.

- **Communication:** Need free email hosting? Zoho has you covered with Zoho Mail. Need to speak to one of you reps right away? Send IM's with Zoho Cliq.

- **Collaboration:** Zoho is the team leader when it comes to, well, leading your team. Start with Zoho Projects to keep track of your projects and finish with Zoho Bug Tracker to kill off any pesky bugs and issues that might have wandered into your process. If you have an agile team of software nerds, have them take a look at Zoho Sprints. Zoho One will also let you host online Meetings and Webinars.

- **Productivity:** Everyone needs a word processor and a

spreadsheet product and Zoho One includes Zoho Writer and Zoho Sheet to provide you with these important tools. And of course, Zoho Workdrive allows you to share documents with the rest of your organization, while Zoho Sign allows you to snag electronic signatures.

- **Finance:** Everyone's least favorite topic becomes easier. You can use the standalone apps like Zoho Invoice to send invoices and collect payment, or Zoho Books to have an accounting system that is fully integrated with your CRM.
- **Operations:** Need a bit of help with your backend processes? Take a look at Zoho Subscription Management to automate your recurring billing, or Zoho Inventory Management to create a centralized inventory management system.
- **HR:** If you are the designated HR person, be sure to check out Zoho People. And, if you're a recruiter, check out Zoho Recruit.
- **Business Process:** By now you have certainly seen the value in Zoho One. However, just to make sure that and have everything you could ever hope for, Zoho One includes tools like Zoho Creator to develop your own custom applications and Zoho Analytics to create business intelligence level reports and dashboards.

You can sign up for a 30-day trial of Zoho One at **TechBenders.com/One**.

You Can Take It with You

Sales people, by nature, are very often out and about. And, with the advent of COVID-19, more and more employees are working from home. Zoho users expect to access their applications from anywhere and everywhere, and from a variety of devices.

Virtually all of the Zoho apps can be accessed from your computer, your smart phone, and your tablet. On mobile devices, simply download the app, login, and your information is available to you in real time.

You might even find that you use different apps on different devices for different purposes. For example, most users find that they are more comfortable running Zoho CRM from their work computer. However, you might want to pull out your phone and get a bit of work done using Zoho Card Scanner and Zoho Expense while waiting for a flight. Or you might find yourself using Zoho

Social from your iPad while watching the tube at night.

Zoho Expense

Congratulations! You flew out to Denver, closed a big deal, and now you are sitting in the airport relaxing with a well-deserved glass of wine. But wait! It's the end of the month and your expense report is due tomorrow. And if you don't get the latest batch of expenses logged in, you'll have to wait another month to get reimbursed.

Enter Zoho Expense, an online expense reporting software that automates expense report creation, streamlines approvals, and makes it easy to get reimbursed quickly. Zoho Expense makes it easy to stay on top of your expenses, whether you are at the office or on the road. Simply photograph expenses into your phone as they happen and Zoho Expense automatically saves details like the date, cost, and business name. Zoho Expense can be used as a stand alone product, or it integrates with Zoho Books. If you need Zoho QuickBooks integration, Zoho Expense integrates with both QuickBooks Online and QuickBooks desktop.

Alternatively, if you are working from your office, you can attach a receipt, enter the cost, and pin the expense to an expense report. You can even do a bulk addition of expenses. Zoho Expense reports can be sorted by expense, category, or date, and you can easily add notes to any expense. Businesses can create and allot per diem expense rates for their employees to ensure that no one spends beyond the allowed limit.

Zoho Expense costs a mere $2.50/user/month. Zoho Expense is included with Zoho One, or can be purchased separately by signing up at **TechBenders.com/Expense**.

Begin with Bigin

Zoho CRM and Zoho One are extremely comprehensive products. This book assumes that you want the whole enchilada and will use a majority of the features. On the other hand, you may fit into one of the following categories and be looking for a solution that is both basic and inexpensive. Other times, users belong to one of these categories and are looking for a solution that is very basic and inexpensive:

- ➢ A start-up that just needs very basic CRM functionality but may lack the funds to subscribe to Zoho CRM.
- ➢ Anyone who has a bunch of private contacts that they want to keep separate from the company database.

➤ Someone who is retiring and just needs very basic contact management.

I have found one product that is extremely functional and inexpensive: Zoho Bigin. For those "financially sensitive" users in the crowd, the cost of Zoho Bigin is $9/month, or a mere $84/year when paid in advance.

The Bigin price tag might be small, but its feature set is impressive and includes:

- ➤ Multiple pipelines
- ➤ Built in telephony
- ➤ Workflow automation
- ➤ Real-time notifications
- ➤ Customizable Dashboards
- ➤ GSuite, Office 365, and Twitter integration

Needless to say, Bigin is fully mobile and accessible from your mobile devices.

And yes, you can easily upgrade Bigin to Zoho CRM if you outgrow the Bigin functionality. You can upgrade existing Bigin records to Zoho CRM with the click of a button and continue to grow your business without any interruption.

If your needs are super simple and you have less than 500 contacts, there is a free edition of Zoho Bigin. Or, at the risk of sounding like a broken record, Bigin is included with Zoho One. To sign up for Bigin, go to **TechBenders.com/Bigin**.

Adding Your Contacts to Your Mobile Device

All of your contacts are readily accessible on your phone if you use the Zoho CRM app. However, many users prefer to have their Zoho contacts sync directly to their phone's native Address book so they can take advantage of the functionality that comes with their smart phone, including caller ID. This is done through a process called CardDav, which is an Internet protocol for syncing contacts.

Both Android and Apple phones use the CardDav protocol and the setup for both phone types is fairly similar.

CardDAV for iOS

Here is the step-by-step process to synchronize contacts from your iPhone with Zoho Contacts:

1. Go to **Settings** on your iPhone.
2. Click **Contacts** and and then choose **Accounts**.
3. Click **Add Account** and choose **Other.**
4. Click **Add CardDAV Account** and then enter the **Server address** as *Contacts.Zoho.com*.
5. Fill in your **Username** and **Password**.
6. Click **Next**. All your contacts will be synchronized.

CardDAV for Android

To sync your Android contacts with your Zoho Contacts, you will have to install a free app called **CardDAV-Sync free** from the Google Play store.

Follow these steps to configure the CardDAV-Sync free app:

1. Open the app and choose the **CardDAV** option.
2. Click **Add account.**
3. Enter the following URL as the *Server* name: **https://contacts.zoho.com/carddav.**
4. Enter your **Username** and **Password** and then click **Next**.

Once the app is configured, you can view your Zoho Contacts in the Android Contacts app.

15

Help, Please

I am often asked how long it takes to master Zoho. That's a really tough question. We all learn differently. You might just need the basics, or perhaps the sky is the limit. You might be a visual learner and prefer to read documentation. Maybe you prefer to take a more hands-on approach and tinker with a program as a way of learning. Or you might require a bit more hand-holding and prefer to have someone directly show you the ropes.

I tried to organize this book in a logical progression. You may skip the chapters that don't pertain to you or your business. I know you may still have a ton of questions. Hopefully, this chapter helps you find the answers - no matter what your learning style!

In addition to the information that I provide in this book, Zoho offers a variety of sources that supply step-by-step instructions for just about any feature that you might want to explore. If need a few more resources, this chapter lists several of my favorite learning spots.

Start by Taking a Good Look at Yourself

A great place to start your quest for knowledge is right in Zoho. If you click your profile picture in the top right corner of Zoho's horizontal Navigation Bar, you find a few valuable tidbits of information lurking in your Profile page.

Zoho Support

All Zoho accounts include free support. The My Account tab of your Profile page includes three ways to contact support:

- ✓ Chat with us: Strike up an instant conversation with one of the Zoho support gurus.
- ✓ Write to us: Click this to email Zoho support quicker than you can say Help!
- ✓ Talk to us: I am often asked for Zoho's customer support number. Click the headset icon and you can easily access the number for Zoho's tech support.

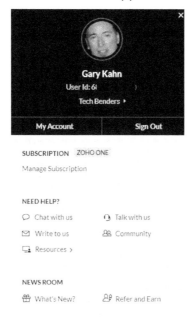

Fig 15-1 Support Screen

Find Out What's New

Zoho is sassy – or at least considered SaaS (software as a service). From time-to-time, Zoho will ask you if you would like to add new features into Zoho. Many will add them sight unseen, which is fine. The changes generally appear in your notifications. However, if you want the full 411 on everything that's new and exciting in the world of Zoho, click the What's New hyperlink and you are transported to a page that tells you about the most recent changes in great detail.

Resources

> **Videos:** This may not be Netflix but it is an easy way to get to hours of free Zoho video tutorials.

> **Documentation:** Zoho offers an abundance of articles in its extensive and continually updated knowledge base. You can link to many of these how-tos here – and save a few trees along the way.

> **Training**: The Zoho team offers a plethora of training opportunities, both in person and online. Click here to learn about the latest and greatest classes that are available.

> **More:** I love a company that thinks of everything, which must explain why I like Zoho so much. Clicking this option will send you on your way to a whole lot of other resources.

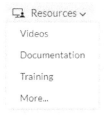

Fig 15-2 Zoho Resources

We Get by With a Little Help from Our Friends

Zoho users come from all over the world. But all Zoho users share a few things in common: they love Zoho and want to learn as much as they can about the products. And trust me, there's an awful lot of knowledge to be learned! Click on the **Community** option to search through issues that have been presented by other users – or post a question or two of your own.

I Need an eBook (or two)

A picture may be worth a thousand words, but I'd rather have the thousand words when it comes to researching a problem. There are way more than a thousand words available to you on the Zoho website. Like I said before, everyone learns in a different way. I am assuming that if you purchased this book you like to learn from a book. To download free eBooks and access a range of topics to get deeper insight on successfully using Zoho CRM go to ***https://www.Zoho.com/crm/resources/ebooks***.

Zoho CRM Training Programs and Webinars

Although it doesn't offer a tree-lined campus and a great football team like my Alma Mater (Go, Gators!), the various Zoho webinars offer a great curriculum of courses designed to increase your knowledge of Zoho at a very rapid pace. And unlike other universities, most of the webinars are free - as in no tuition!

Learn how to use the best tools for automating your sales process and better customer engagement from Zoho's implementation specialists by registering for a class here: ***https://www.Zoho.com/crm/customer-success***.

Pressed for time? Many of the webinars are posted online, and some webinars are repeated on an ongoing basis. Sign up for a webinar and learn the Zoho CRM basics, from customization to sales process automation and more by going to ***https://www.Zoho.com/crm/webinars***.

Join a Local Zoho Users Group (ZUG)

Talk about a global community! Zoho User Groups are located on 6 continents, 30 countries, 100+ cities, and have over 10,000 members. Join a ZUG near you to meet, network, and share ideas with other Zoho users, Zoho product experts, and local partners. To find a group close to you go to ***https://community.Zoho.com/user-groups.***

For me, the jury is out on this tip about tips. Still, you might get bored one day and decide that you just have to learn one new thing about Zoho. If that's the case, head over to the **Zoho CRM Tips** website where you are bound to find a nugget or two. Who knows? You might just uncover that one in a million tip that will save your hours of time – or make you millions of dollars! To check out the tips go to ***https://www.Zoho.com/crm/resources/tips/#all***.

Become an Official Zoholic

Zoholics is an annual live event which is designed to give you the opportunity to learn, network, and get the resources needed to take your team to the next level. In this event you'll hear about the latest Zoho solutions, get inspired by the visionary keynotes, experience hands-on workshops and one-on-one sessions, and connect with like-minded people who also use Zoho to drive their businesses. These events are held in locations around the world including the United States, Canada, Latin America, Europe, Israel and even Africa. Quite frankly, the US Zoholics event held annually in Austin, Texas, is a great way to learn more about Zoho – and have a whole lot of fun in the bargain!

Hire a Zoho Consultant

Many years ago, I decided to wallpaper my living room - I chose very expensive (and thin!) paper. Not wanting to drip paste on my carpet, I set up a table in my garage for the pasting process, smeared on the paste, and carted the gooey paper into the dining room. Those of you who have ever tried their luck at wallpapering can imagine the results. For the rest of you, picture a mummy wrapped in a lovely print and you'll get the drift. Once I had removed the paper and paste from various parts of my anatomy, I sheepishly called in an expert. Mr. Expert gave me a few strange looks, muttered about the table in the garage, and had my dining room done in no time.

You might find yourself in a similar situation when learning Zoho. Perhaps you don't have the time - or patience - to attend a class or read documentation. Maybe you have specific questions about functionality as it applies to your business. For whatever the reason, you might want to hire an expert to help you with some, or all, of your installation.

Zoho Partners are experts who earn their living helping folks like you implement Zoho. Consultants can customize Zoho to your specific situation, train your employees on all of the Zoho functionality, align your company's processes to Zoho, and help setup automated procedures. Full disclosure: in addition to being the author of this book I am also a Zoho Partner. You can reach me at **info@TechBenders.com**

Develop a Sense of Community

Some of you like to do things on your own. That's probably why you picked up this book in the first place! However, you might find yourself scratching your head trying to figure something out. You are not alone! There are millions of Zoho users, many of which like to help out other users. If you would like to take part in the Zoho Community forums go to https://help.zoho.com/portal/en/community.

Index

A

Account 196, 198
Agents 150
Anomaly Detector 175
Attachment 53, 105, 178
Auto-Number 61

B

Big Deal Alert 121
Big Deal Rule 122
Bigin 195
Blueprint 93
Books 99
Business Card 77

C

Campaigns 3
CardDav 195
Case 183
Classic Home Page 162
Click Rate 107
Cliq 187
Clone 14, 83, 106, 122
Cohort 175
Community 200
Comparator 174
Components 162
Contact 115
Convert Button 12
CRM Ground Rules 5
CRM Tool 2

D

Dashboards 174
Database Backup 96
Database 123
Deal 115
Deal Amount 118
Departments 150
Desk 149
Draft Mode 129
Drop-Down 181
Duplicates 36

E

Ellipsis Button 67
Email 101
Email Attachment 178
Enterprise Edition 101
Expected Revenue 121
Exporting 179
Exporting Records 179

F

Favorite Reports 171
Field 2
File Upload 62
Find and Replace 33
Formula 62
Funnel 175

G

Global Search 16

H

Home 161

I

Image 62
Inventory 193

K

K

Kanban 29
Karen Fredricks 205
Karen's Four Rules 6
KB 155, 157, 158
KB Articles 158
Knowledge Base 147
KPI 143

L

Layout 75
Lead 162
Leads Module 12, 37, 64
Left Navigation Bar 183
Lookup Field 73

M

Mass Update 35
Matrix Report 166
Member Accounts Related 19
Milestone 137
Module 2
Modules Bar 54
Multiple Pipelines 116
Multi-Select Lookup Field 18

N

New Layout 79

O

Open Rate 107, 112

P

Parent Account 19
Pick List 60
Pipeline 195
Probability 118
Products 205
Professional Edition 101
Profile 7, 65, 70, 197, 198
Project Calendar 145
Project issue 138
Projects 141
Projects List 144

Q

Quadrant 175
QuickBooks 4, 126
Quick Create Layouts 76
Quotes 127

R

Record 2
Related Lists 78
Reports 165
Report Scheduler 169
Role 13
RouteIQ 186

S

Sales Pipeline 116
Save Time 126
Search 21
Section 177
Setup Gear 112
Sheet View 178, 179
Slack 187
Speed Tasking 136
Standard Edition 101
Subform 74
Summary Report 165, 168
Super Admin 82
Support 4, 147, 192, 205
Survey 53, 184, 185

T

Tab Groups 164
Tabular Report 165
Tabular View 163
Target Meter 175
Task 45
Task List 141
Task List Template 141
Template 141
Templated Email 107
Template Gallery 102
Ticket 152
Transition 150

U

User 81

W

Wizard 180
Workflow Rules 91
Work Overview 145

Z

Zoho Analytics 180
Zoho Apps 4
Zoho Books 4
Zoho Campaigns 113
Zoho Consultants 201
Zoho CRM 1
Zoho CRM Ground Rules 5
Zoho Desk 149
Zoho Docs 178
Zoho Expense 124
Zoho Finance Suite 124
Zoho Flavor 3
Zoholic 200
Zoho Meetings 4
Zoho Modules 4
Zoho One 7
ZohoPaloozza 177

Zoho Partners 201
Zoho Projects 139
Zoho Sheet View 180
Zoho Sign 4
Zoho Survey 184

About Karen Fredricks

Karen Fredricks began her life rather non-technically growing up in Kenya. She attended high school in Beirut, Lebanon, where she developed her sense of humor while dodging bombs. Having traveled all over the world, she ended up at the University of Florida and has been an ardent Gator fan ever since. In addition to undergraduate studies in English and Accounting, Karen has a Master's degree in Psycholinguistics. Karen began her career teaching high school English and Theatre. She has worked with the PC since its inception in the early 80's and has worked as a full-time CRM consultant and trainer ever since.

Karen is the author of thirteen books on CRM and Contact Management Software, including eleven "**For Dummies**" titles. Her works include titles on ACT, Outlook, SugarCRM, Outlook Business Contact Manager, and Microsoft Office Live. She created training videos on Outlook and ACT! for LinkedIn Learning. A true CRM fanatic, she is the founder of the Virtual CRM Users Group and holds frequent webinars focusing on CRM usage.

Karen's company, Tech Benders, provides consulting, support, and training services for a variety of CRM products. She has worked with numerous Fortune 500 companies and other well-known entities including the PGA, the ATP, Florida Power & Light, and Volvo of North America. Her focus is on making companies more efficient and productive – and therefore more profitable.

A Boca Raton resident for over 30 years, Karen spends her spare time playing tennis, running to the gym, and walking on the beach.

Karen can be reached at **Info@TechBenders.com**

CPSIA information can be obtained
at www.ICGtesting.com
Printed in the USA
BVHW052035150522
636460BV00008B/130